HER 12TH YEAR:

She's Not So Little Anymore

Parental Coaching Guide for Raising Tweens (11-14)

By Dr. Lisa T. Sistrunk, EdD.

Her 12th Year: She's Not So Little Anymore
by Dr. Lisa T. Sistrunk

Books may be purchased by contacting the publisher and author at:
http://www.Her12thYear.com
Editor: **Attiyya Atkins, A+ Editing & Content Creation**

ISBN: 978-1-7366769-0-5
Printed in USA

About the Author

Dr. Lisa is a wife, mother, sister, life coach, and human development and leadership professional. She's a practitioner in helping people *"elevate their ordinary,"* (even when raising a tween or teen). Dr. Lisa wrote "Her 12th Year: She's Not So Little Anymore" based out of the real conversations and experiences that created a bond of open communication and trust between her daughter, Kamaria (k-Mar-ree-a) Joy, and her.

Dr. Lisa has obtained her Doctoral degree in Organizational Leadership and Development from Grand Canyon University, her Master's in Adult Education from Central Michigan University and undergrad from Adelphi University. The CEO of Metro Atlanta-based, DH Elevation Consulting, Dr. Lisa is a national and international master trainer and motivational speaker. She has coached and mentored clients from 13 to 75 years young. Dr. Lisa's passion is guiding young adults (17-30 year old's) into becoming healthy leaders of their own lives as they journey into adulthood. When not coaching or writing, Dr. Lisa, along with her husband Mark, enjoy exploring national parks and European castles, and hosting backyard bonfires for family and friends. Born and raised in Hartford, Connecticut, then moving to Georgia after graduating college, Dr. Lisa likes to say she is a Georgia Peach covered in Nutmeg.

"Her 12th Year" is the first book but will not be the last. You are invited to join the "12th Year Community" at **www.Her12thYear.com**.

You can also check out her @Dhelevation on YouTube Channel *"Elevate Your Ordinary"*, IG, Facebook, LinkedIn & Twitter; & @DrLisa_dhe on Tik Tok.

My Hopes for This Book

- To encourage intentional conversations that build a

  foundation strengthening the thoughts and actions of girls entering their teen

  years.

- To increase trust, honesty, openness, and love between parents and daughters.

I have written this guide, primarily, in the voice in which I spoke to my daughter, and as you may speak to your daughter. I offer my words as suggestions. I hope this book helps you find your voice, especially on topics that are difficult to talk about. There will be places where I speak directly to you are the parent. I have provided real stories, *in italics*, for application. Feel free to use your own relevant stories to connect and make the topics come alive in a more personal way, or you may want to share or have your daughter read my daughter's *"Kamaría story,"* which is highlighted throughout.
I have provided space for a "Journal Entry" at the end of each conversation. Here you can jot thoughts or stories you want to share with your daughter or write reflections or comments from your talks. If your daughter is 11 or 12, you may want to note your observations of her now and then have follow-up talks with her when she's 13 or 14 and write notes of how she may have grown.

Dedication

The 12th Year is first dedicated to my late parents, Benjamin H. Tillman, III and Joyce JP Tillman. How I wish you both were here to celebrate this with us. This is because of the memories of the love, time, and energy you both put into being our parents. From ensuring we had a strong spiritual foundation to making sure we were grounded in family, we appreciate you. You volunteered at school so much the other kids thought you worked there. It's because of you attending my basketball and softball games, watching us cheer and dance, and taking us on long Saturday drives around New England that I wanted to make sure Kamaria would be able to look back on her childhood with the same loving feelings. I feel your presence daily. See you in my dreams!

Next, this book is of course dedicated to my mini-me, Kamaria Joy. You truly are the joy in my heart. Being your mom is one of my greatest thrills and accomplishments! While not always easy nor fun, I would not trade our life together for anything. I appreciate all that is you. Thank you for allowing me to share a part of our journey with the readers. Continue developing into the amazing, loving, and devoted woman of God you are. Your shine can never be dulled! ILYMTL Punkin'.

Finally, this book is dedicated to the daughters who are longing to hear from and talk with their parents, whether they realize it or not. It's their hearts, spirits, and minds that we cultivate with each conversation, each tear we wipe, each hug and laugh we share. Parenting doesn't come with instructions, it is not always rewarding, and it sure can be exhausting! As parents, we don't always get it right, we can be embarrassing and confusing at times. But *parenting is worth it all* to help our children become the best they can be. Because we love them, we need to have these meaningful conversations to guide them through life.

Acknowledgements

Truly a family affair!

No accomplishment in my life would be possible without the unfailing love of my Heavenly Father. Fifteen years ago, He started me on this journey and has seen it to completion. I continue to stand on your promises.

I could not have completed this book without the love and support of my wonderful husband, Mark. You proofread for me, listened to me, read aloud, were patient the many nights I didn't come to bed so I could write "one more section," and were always cheering me on to completion. You are my gift that I treasure daily. You are my heart.

To my sister, the author and spoken word artist, Brenda "BMichelle" Tillman who paved the way for me with *"Shades of Mandingo," "Listen: Your Inner Voice,"* and *"Happy! Happy! Happy!"* Your love, creative energy, and invaluable experience and suggestions helped make this possible. Your pride, encouragement and support mean all the world to me! Look at us! Sister authors! I love you, big sister!

Cass the Artist, my niece Cassandra J Sistrunk, thank you for taking on the task of creating the cover art. You were able to capture by verbal vision and make it a visual reality. You really are the Dope Art Queen!

For the moms, dads, former tweens and those who work with tweens, and who agreed to read the manuscript and beta test, I thank you so much. Your feedback let me know that this was truly heart work worth completing. It is my prayer and hope that your connections with your girls grow deeper daily.

To Attiyya Atkins of A Plus Editing, thank you for your professionalism, finishing touches and guidance which helped finalize my dream!

Reviews

"You covered all of the things I would have loved to have communicated with my parents about... It's a great guide for those who want to develop a better relationship with their daughters." -Priscilla Harris, Sr. Technology Consultant.

"It's a great mother/daughter book to read going into middle school and going into high school."
-Jessica Hardy, Mom of 12-year-old and founder and spokesperson for Single Moms Group.

What you are conveying in your writings, speak to helping the countless parents that do and will continue to fall into the trap of believing that" well they don't listen anyway", or their still young, these conversations can wait" (I was one of those dads unfortunately). - Steve Browning, M.ED. Dad of 3 & Grandfather of 3; Associate Pastor; Chair & President, Fathers for Scholars, Inc.; Certified Relationship Coach; Child Welfare Professional

"It helps you to realize that your child is not going through these changes alone and neither are you!" -Dr. Jawanna Smith Wilkins, Mom of a 14-year-old.

"I was impressed at the unapologetic ferocity of your mothering..."-Ann Perry Wallace, Mom of 11- and 16-year old.

"10 out of 10,"
-Dr. James C. Rodriquez, Single Dad, President & CEO of Fathers & Families Coalition of America

Introduction

This book is a direct result of 48 individual conversations I had with my daughter over the 52 weeks of her 12th year of life. She is 27 now. I left four weeks without a topic as I knew I would need to repeat a few of them.

The making of the original list of topics came from my own apprehension. I feared that my daughter, who would soon be a teenager, would stop listening to me over her peers. There were things I still wanted and needed to teach her while I was still the primary influence in her life. Additionally, as a mom, middle school was scary for me. There had been news reports and articles about a "game" involving multi-colored jelly bracelets that middle schoolers were wearing. If a boy or girl popped your bracelet, you were supposed to perform a sexual act with them. Each color had a different act, ranging from a kiss to full sexual intercourse! Shocking!

Let me remind you we are talking about children, 11 to 14 years old, doing these things. I'm sure you can see why I was concerned. As I relive that time, I still feel a bit of angst.

 For all of these years, my baby, my mini-me, my sidekick, hung on my words. The possibility that other children, whom I didn't know because we moved to a new city, would or could have this type of interaction or influence on my child was inconceivable!

I knew I needed to act fast, but to do what and how?

Recognizing my baby would soon be turning 12, my mind was telling me, "I have 52 weeks to make an impression." I prayed, thought, and then began my plan.

This guide is written to parents, guardians, aunties, uncles, mentors, and other adults who want to help their budding teen develop healthy thoughts and skills. This book will help our adolescents not fall into some of the traps we may have fallen into during this pivotal stage in our lives. These are starter conversations. They are not one and done. You may find yourself revisiting these topics throughout their teen years and maybe into early adulthood.

You may find some of the talks uncomfortable. That's just natural. There is no growth without discomfort. I encourage you to lean into the discomfort. Work through it. Breathe through it. Don't shy away. You may start talking, then find it necessary to stop, regroup and come back. Some of you may want to pray or meditate before initiating some or all of the topics.

You purchased this guide for a reason. And that reason is growing fast before your eyes. Please continue to help her be all that she can be in the best way she can be. Give her the tools to know that she can make wise decisions and have the confidence to know she can talk to you about anything without judgment and lies.

This guide is filled with quotes, definitions, and personal stories of how I took my daughter on this journey. After each characteristic or skill, there is a place for you to journal your notes, questions, comments, or resources.

The conversations may get *REAL*. In fact, they *SHOULD GET REAL*. Be patient with yourself and your daughter. I found these conversations to be worthwhile and enlightening for my daughter and me, and they helped solidify the bonds of trust and open communication we share today, 15 years later.

Foreword

For as long as I could remember my friends loved my mom. Many of them told me I was lucky to have her. Although as a kid I thought she was standard (lol) and everyone had a mom like her. A mom who gave them lots of attention and love, but still put them on punishment for no reason. I've grown up to realize that close mother/daughter bonds are sacred and not always the norm. I am so thankful for the safe space my mother created for us to have an open dialogue about these necessary coming of age conversations.

As a tween, I thought these conversations were HIGHLY awkward and uncomfortable, especially the one about sex (omg). However, as I grew into my teen, and then young adult, years, I knew there was nothing I couldn't tell my mother. It was only a few years ago when she jokingly told me she could no longer be my life coach and hear my adult shenanigans and that instead, I needed a therapist.

That is my mom to a T! A loving, guiding woman whose experience I've only ever been able to glean wisdom from, whether I used it or not. There is no doubt her guidance made me a better, wiser, and healthier woman.

My hope after reading "Her 12th Year..." is that the bond between parents and daughters are strengthened, and encouraged to foster a relationship of honesty, love, and trust on their own terms for years to come. I am praying for generations of healthy parent/child relationships from the 11th year and beyond. All the love and all the best,

XO- KJ

Table of Contents

Chapter 1 – Character

The mental and moral qualities distinctive to an individual[3]

You can never escape your character. It is always with you, good, bad, or indifferent. It is the foundation of who you are. While you will make mistakes and poor choices along the way – it does not change who you are at your core, and who you and others know you to be. I wanted Kamaria to be of good character. That is what most parents want. Your character will carry you far, in the classroom, on the ball field, with your friends and family, and eventually in your place of work. It's who you are, the way you act, whether someone is looking or not. And a not-so-secret secret is that nowadays, everyone is looking and usually recording!

Integrity & Honesty: Honesty means telling the truth, while Integrity means doing the right thing, whether it benefits you or not.[1]

"Oh, sweet girl, don't worry about being merely beautiful. Be bold. Be wild. Be strong. Be confident. Be independent and intelligent. Be fierce. Be brave enough to be real in this fake world. Redefine beauty." -Brooke Hampton

Begin small. Develop your integrity within yourself. Be true to what you say you will and will not do for yourself, towards your family members and close friends. You don't have to make any grand announcement about your actions and deeds. Just do it and recognize your own efforts. Smile at yourself and know that you are more than capable of trusting yourself. Far too many of us don't trust ourselves. When you can trust yourself, it builds your confidence. This, in turn, shines through in your words and actions towards others. While some may not be able to define that light that shines in you, they will be attracted to it as you become someone they can relate to and depend on.

Kamaria had an issue with lying, so we had the "Clean Slate" talk. The talk went something like this: A clean slate is like a cleaned chalkboard/whiteboard. All that was written on it has been erased. It is a fresh start for new things to be written and created. So, let's start over. All the things you have been dishonest about in the past are wiped away...Never to be brought up again.

Side note: Doesn't it sound like a very familiar story another Father tells His children?

Back to the convo: *As your mom, I love you and believe in the good in you. This is a chance for us to reconnect and rebuild the trust between us. I will always be here for you, no matter what you do. If you do wrong, it is my responsibility to address it. But to address it best, I have to know that I can trust you are telling me the truth. I will always have your back. You can trust me to be in your corner. Now that doesn't mean that I will cover up for you nor allow you to get away with any wrong. But what it does mean is that I will fight for the best for and in you. If something happens...you cheat on a test, you know something about a situation that was bad... come to me, tell me the truth, and we will handle it together. As long as we have the truth we can build from there.*

While this may seem like a stretch for some of you, as you may think you are too far gone from the honesty department. There is still some hope in you, and in your parents.

<u>Parents</u> if your child is in a juvenile detention center. Know that if you and your child still have breath, there is still a chance to rebuild the trust.

You are not developing integrity for your parents. This is for you. You will always be in your own presence. As you get older, you will do what all of us have done, grow away from your parents and exert your independent lives.

We often don't want our children to do things just because we said so (I always hated when my dad or mom would say that...I wanted to know why... more about that later in the Communication chapter). As I said earlier, developing trust within yourself builds confidence in your judgments and decision-making skills. These skills are vitally important to being a healthy and well-adjusted person. Knowing that you can be trusted and are worthy of others trust is a character trait worth striving for.

Journal Entry:

Kindness: Being friendly, generous, and considerate.[2]

"We can't heal the world today, but we can begin with a voice of compassion, a heart of love, and an act of kindness." -Mary Davis

When Kamaria was in the 1st grade, one of her classmates, who was mildly autistic, was having difficulty completing an in-class assignment. KJ as I call her, stopped what she was doing to make sure he was okay and knew what to do. When the teacher noticed, she got on KJ for talking in class and not doing her own work. Kamaria tried to explain that she was helping him out, but the teacher told her to get back to her seat. Later that evening, Kamaria was still sad about the situation. When I asked her why she decided to stop doing her work to help him instead of finishing her work first as they were instructed, she matter of factly told me "because he needed the help then." Kamaria didn't care about the consequences of stopping her work. She felt his needs were more important. While I explained the importance of her following directions, I also told her that her selflessness meant a lot to her classmate and me. I also agreed that sometimes you have to sacrifice yourself for what you believe in for the sake of others.

While acts of kindness do not always come with reprimand, they do require you to get outside of yourself for the sake of another. *The kind heart Kamaria displayed in the first grade continued to show up as she grew into a middle schooler. We lived in the suburbs but attended church downtown. When we had to go to a choir rehearsal or Sunday service, if there was food in the car, no matter if it was homemade or fast food, or if she was hungry or not, she often wanted to share whatever we had with a homeless person we might be driving by. One Sunday, we had just picked up some fast food and she was enjoying one of her two biscuit sandwiches. When she spotted a homeless man at the next corner. She asked if she could share her meal. I drove up to him and she handed him her second biscuit and hash browns. She then said, "I ate half of this, but you can have it and split the other with your friend." The gentleman smiled and thanked her. Now my daughter loves to eat! So, for her to share the food in her hand was a supreme act of selflessness!*

Acts of kindness can be small for the giver, yet very meaningful to the receiver. Helping with chores at home without being asked; a genuine smile given to a stranger you pass; sharing a warm embrace (with both arms) to let someone know you are happy to see them; leaving a note under a windshield wiper to say have a nice day; holding the door for the person behind you and wishing them a good day... you get the idea. Kindness starts with being kind to yourself, in words and actions.

Instead of bad talking yourself because you did poorly on a test or didn't make the winning shot, tell yourself you will prepare better starting today or that you will practice harder or ask the coach for extra help. Kindness also begins at home. Help out without being asked, do something you aren't expected to do. Let those closest to you know that they matter to you by being kind. Then find ways to be kind outside of your house. A little kindness goes a long way. It also makes you feel better about yourself and life in general. It is a character trait that can be nurtured and learned in each of us. As you show kindness to others, kindness flows back to you.

Journal Entry:

Respect: admiring someone or something so deeply due to their abilities, qualities, or achievements.[3]

Respect of Self:
"Don't underestimate me because I'm quiet. I know more than I say. I think more than I speak. And I observe more than you know." -Whisper

As Kamaria was developing her own style and voice, I would often remind her that how she treated and presented herself is how others will learn how to treat and interact with her. That if she was sloppy and unkempt; if she turned in assignments with her name scribbled and the paper crumpled or torn; or if she talked down about herself, others are more likely to follow her lead and not expect much from her efforts. They may not give her their best or may use words that are less than positive or encouraging when referring to her. I reminded her that she sets the tone and standard for herself.

How you show up in the world is how the world will show up to you. We plant seeds in the universe with our thoughts, words, and deeds and what grows is a direct result of that. What you put out is what you will get back. That doesn't mean that what you get back is what you deserve. It simply means to take care of you and all that represents you. You can only control you, and I encourage you to do so with care and intention to get the best results out of life.

Respect of Others:
"Sisters function as safety in a chaotic world simply by being there for each other." -Carol Saline

There was an incident when Kamaria was upset with a friend. All she knew was that her friend acted "funny" towards her and she didn't like it. I asked Kamaria if she talked to her friend about it. She said, "no, my friend should say something if there was a problem." I shared that things are not always as they seem and that if she really valued their friendship, she should find out what was going on. I told her that doing so couldn't hurt since they were already not talking much. Kamaria wasn't too interested in that idea. However, two days later, she finally decided to ask her friend what was up. To her surprise, the girl said she was hurt because she really needed to talk with Kamaria earlier in the week (around the same time she was reportedly acting "funny"), but Kamaria was being standoffish. She wanted and needed her friend to hear her and to be there for her regarding a situation at home, but instead her friend was in her own emotions and not receptive.

I often say that my mind can be a scary place if left to its own devices. I have been known to come up with all sorts of strange and not so pleasant ideas when I start filling in blanks to unanswered questions. I imagine that Kamaria and I are not the only ones that have done this. Oddly enough, asking questions and listening is the easiest and most difficult thing to do. We need to open our ears, not our assumptions, to those we care about. We need to take the time to find out how our friends are doing. If they share, great! If not, that's ok too. At least they know you are there, and you cared enough to clear the air. That's all you can do.

Journal Entry:

Loyalty: a strong sense of support or allegiance.[3]

"Loyalty isn't grey, it's black and white. You're either completely loyal, or not loyal at all." -Sharnay

I taught my daughter that loyalty means something. First being loyal to yourself and your values, then loyal to your family and friends. But just because someone is a relative doesn't mean they deserve your loyalty.

As with most kids, Kamaria had a close friend from early elementary school who she liked to hang out with. As the girls got older, they began developing different interests. One of the girl's new interests was something that Kamaria did not feel comfortable with, but she thought she had to like it to keep her friend. I didn't hear about this situation until after KJ was out of middle school. But I was pleased to learn that though she initially agreed to participate in the activity, she decided to stay true to herself when it came time. She said it was not easy to tell her friend that she had changed her mind, but she was glad she did it.

Loyalty is earned, like trust (which we will get into next). It develops from the good and not so good times you share with someone. It develops from knowing what you believe in and stand for and then aligning yourself with others who believe the same or similar things. As we continually grow and change so do many of our beliefs. So, we must check in with ourselves from time to time to make sure we are in tune with our own beliefs and have not just latched on to someone else's.

Journal Entry:

Honesty & Trust: Honesty refers to a facet of moral character and connotes positive and virtuous attributes such as integrity, truthfulness, straightforwardness, including straightforwardness of conduct, along with the absence of lying, cheating, theft, etc.[20]

"No matter how plain a woman may be, if truth and honesty are written across her face, she will be beautiful." -Eleanor Roosevelt

Early on Kamaria and I established the importance of me trusting her and vice versa. She knew she could come to me, good, bad, or indifferent, with anything because we established mutual trust. One important thing she knew about me was that if she did something wrong, I needed to hear it from her first, rather than from "the streets." She would still have consequences for her bad behavior if she told me, but the punishment would likely not be as severe if the incident came from her mouth rather than the mouths of others. Now, I am not saying her ability to come to me or my ability to hear her was always easy. But we worked through those challenging times, and they have certainly been worth it.

One situation sticks out prominently in my mind from her seventh-grade year. Late morning, on a school day, I received a text from KJ. This was the first odd thing because she was in school and should not have been on her phone. With concern, I opened the text, which said, "Mom, have you ever cheated on a test in school?" Now, that was the second odd thing! I looked at the text, wondering why I was getting such a question. Before I had even two minutes to think, the next text appeared saying, "I need to know now please, seriously." So, I rolled my eyes and texted back, "Yes, I have. Why do you ask?" My wonderful, sweet daughter then proceeded to tell me how she knew how important it was for her to pass her test and that she 'didn't want to disappoint me,' so she created a cheat sheet, just in case. Of course, I'm in full eye roll mode at the nerve of this girl trying to put the weight on me for why she didn't properly prepare for her test!

I texted back:

"Oh really?! I'm actually disappointed that you didn't do what you needed to do to pass the test, and then decided to cheat! How are you on your phone? Where are you? And what made you tell me?

She replied that they had a substitute teacher who caught her cheating, took her cheat sheet and test, and ripped them up. A few minutes later KJ asked to go to the bathroom and that's where she had texted me from. I shook my head and rolled my eyes one more time. I let out a heavy sigh then text, "Girl, we will deal with this at home. Get yourself back in class and make better decisions!" She responded with. "Ok. I love you. I'm really sorry." My final words in our conversation, "Don't be sorry, be different!" That's one of my famous character enhancing phrases. We will finish this story up in Chapter 2, under Forgiveness.

Journal Entry:

Actions & Consequences: Action is the process of doing something. A consequence is a "result" or "conclusion," of an action.[4]

"Never blame another person for your personal choices, you are the one who must live out the consequences of your choice." -Caroline Myss

"When you choose an action, you choose the consequences of that action. When you desire a consequence, you had darn* well better take the action that would create it." - Lois McMaster Bujold

As Kamaria started middle school, she began to lose focus on her schoolwork. I am still not fully sure what all went on, but she would do her homework and either forget or simply not turn it in. Talk, fuss and yell as I did, she still didn't have consistency with turning in her assignments. As much as she was making me crazy with this nonsense, I was tired of the struggle and headache.

As she sat across the room from me (believe me, the distance was necessary), I calmly informed her that doing her homework and not handing it in was like me going to work and not submitting my hours to get paid. She understood that her grades were her pay. I shared that her father, teachers, and myself had done our 6th grade work, we passed and graduated high school. That this is completely about her getting what she needed to pass and one day graduate to live the life she wanted to live. I explained that I was tired and wasn't going to fight anymore. If she continued these actions, she would fail the sixth grade. And if that happened, we weren't going to pay for summer school, she would just have to repeat every year until she changed her actions. Then I sent her to her room.

Well, I am not sure which part got to her, but her completing and turning in her assignments was soon a thing of the past. As parents, we truly cannot make you do what you will not do. Sure, some punishments will get your attention and have you comply but ultimately, we want you to understand the reasoning and "get with the program." But we are looking in hindsight and not from where we were when we were your age. You kids can't see what we see from the same perspective. Sometimes you need things clearly spelled out.

I have often heard: 'you just want to be her friend,' 'why are you explaining yourself' or 'you talk too much with her.' Well, I am still the mother she respects at 27. She and I have now become friends and part of that is because we established a strong foundation of communication. But furthermore, over the past 15 years she has developed the ability to make pretty sound decisions due in part to my explanations. I did not want Kamaria to do things just because I said so (well, most of the time). I needed her to develop her decision-making skills that would successfully carry her throughout her life.

Journal Entry:

Chapter 2 - Health & Wellness

Health is a state of being, whereas wellness is the state of living

a healthy lifestyle.[22]

Everyone has physical health, emotional health, mental health, and spiritual health. Each area of health has a range from great to poor. As you grow you are learning more about yourself. As you learn more about yourself you learn how to best care for yourself. Taking time to listen to your body and mind is one way to learn about your health. Your healthcare starts with you, how you treat yourself, and the words you use and thoughts you have about yourself. Your physical health is your activity and what you take into yourself through food, music, pictures, drinks. Before Kamaria was in middle school, I can't say I was intentional about having her listen to her body nor her emotions. But as she grew, and had more emotions to share, the conversations definitely began.

Self-Esteem: Confidence in one's ability and self-worth.[3]

"Beauty begins the moment you decide to be yourself." -Coco Chanel
"Never bend your head. Always hold it high. Look the world straight in the eye." -
Helen Keller

Self-esteem starts in the mind. it is everything you think about yourself and it flows into how you treat and present yourself to the world. *I remember at varying points in my daughter's life talking to her about self-esteem. Things like how to appropriately correct people when they mispronounced her name (except the elders in our family); turning in assignments that were neatly signed (not on water-stained paper); demonstrating her best efforts; having her hair done and clothing presentable for whatever occasion; shaking hands with confidence; believing in herself even when others don't; and speaking positive words to and about herself. These and other specific mindsets and actions I repeated to Kamaria as often as I necessary. I needed her to understand that she sets the tone for herself, both inwardly and outwardly.*

One of the most important self-esteem lessons, that I am thrilled to say she fully continues to live out, is having her presence known when she walks into a room, whether she speaks or not. KJ has honed the ability to walk confidently in who she is no matter where she is. That quiet confidence she carries started to take shape years ago. Our girls were not created to shrink in the presence of boys and men or other girls and women. They shouldn't take whatever is being told to them without healthy questioning, nor believe the glowing words falling from the lips of every sweet talker who comes across their path. Having solid self-esteem, that may waiver upon occasion, serves us all as we develop as healthy individuals.

You will definitely have moments of self-doubt, but when the foundation of solid self-esteem is built, it is easier to pick yourself up again. To shake off the doubt. To find ways to believe in the power of you.

Journal Entry:

Emotions, Moods & Your Cycle: Emotions are short-lived feelings that come from a known cause, while Moods are feelings that are longer lasting than emotions and have no clear starting point of formation.[5]

"I mean if there was any justice in the world you wouldn't even have to go to school on your period. You'd just stay home for five days, eat chocolate and cry." -Andrea Portes

There was a time when Kamaria would get into a funky mood for absolutely no reason. She'd be cranky and have an attitude that would quickly have to be checked. Another of my famous lines heard around the house was "get your life in order!" I would say that often after sending her on her way to her room. I began noticing that she would get like this around the same time every month. It dawned on me that her body was preparing her to start her monthly cycle. While I had already prepped her (and me) for the pending physical changes she would experience, I had not done the same for the possible emotional changes that would come.

Now was the time. I sat her down and asked her to think back over the previous months when I checked her. For her to think if there was something specific that caused her attitudes. She had no real reason why. I then introduced her to "the monkey on her back." I shared that her hormones were changing, and she needed to start paying special attention to manage them. KJ came to learn that the monkey was an unexplained emotional heaviness on her that she couldn't easily shake off. As we talked, we discussed ways to manage herself when this occurred, such as: going to her room to be alone when appropriate; taking extra care in how she spoke to others (taming her tongue); and learning to breathe through the feelings. Mostly, she needed to practice being patient with herself and others during this time. Some months she did better than others and didn't need to be checked.

But as many adults know, managing our mental health is an on-going activity. So, there were definitely other times when I had to play the role of 'attitude adjuster.' With regards to her physical needs during her cycle, Kamaria was taught to have extra pads or tampons in her book bag or purse, be cautious about wearing light colors just in case a leak happens, the proper disposal of her used products, and to keep herself fresh by changing her pads at regular intervals.

Journal Entry:

Personal Appearance: The way that someone or something looks.[3]

"She is clothed in strength and dignity and she laughs without fear of the future." -
Proverbs 31

Like most little girls, KJ loved her baby dolls and wanted to take them everywhere with her. I had two rules: 1. If she could bring a baby, she had to carry her (the "you bring it, you carry it" rule that still holds today) and 2. All babies had to be dressed and have neat hair (after all, I don't take you out of the house naked and with wild hair!).

Among other things, I tried to impress upon her the need to be dressed appropriately. Whether that meant no wrinkles (not looking like you pulled the item from the bottom of the clothes basket), shoes on the right feet and tied, pants zipped and with a belt (if it had loops), no bra straps showing – you get the point. It wasn't that she couldn't get disheveled throughout the day. Heck! There are times when I think being crumpled at the end of the day is a sign of a very good day! But that's not how you should come out of the house in the morning. And while I was no hairstylist and still can't cornrow worth a dime, KJ had multiple neat pigtails with barrettes that matched her outfits or her Grammy, Amora or stepmother cornrowed her hair. It took a village!

The overall world we live in judges at first sight, before you ever open your mouth. Don't give people a reason to turn away from you before they learn how fabulous you are. While you can't control how others think or feel towards you, you can present yourself in a way that says you care about yourself. Remember, self-esteem? Always strive to put your best self forward. And you can start with your smile!

Journal Entry:

Forgiveness of Self & Others: A conscious, deliberate decision to release feelings of resentment or vengeance toward a person or group who has harmed you, regardless of whether they actually deserve your forgiveness. Forgiveness does not mean forgetting, nor does it mean condoning or excusing offenses.[6]

"It's one of the greatest gifts you can give yourself, to forgive. Forgive everyone." - Maya Angelou

The word itself can bring about conflict! Forgiveness has multiple levels: forgiveness *of* others, forgiveness *from* others, and of course, forgiveness of ourselves. It's difficult to select just one experience with my daughter about forgiveness that could possibly cover all levels. So, I will simply share the conversations we had.

Forgive yourself: This is key. *Remember the earlier story when Kamaria cheated on a test and then texted me? Well, here's what happened later that day. I worked from home about half of KJ's school years, and I'm sure this is one of the times she wished I had an office to go to so I wouldn't be there when she got home. I decided not to deal with the situation right away, simply because I just didn't want to expend the energy on it. She came in looking all scared and sad. I hugged and kissed her as usual, told her I had work to finish and we would talk about her day a little later. Then I turned and went back to my desk. Of course, she was not expecting that.*

By the time we talked KJ had more than enough time to think of the entire situation and come up with her own suggestions of punishment (which were far harsher than anything I would have declared). As we talked, and she cried out of her remorse for the entire situation, she accepted her punishment (no cell phone and no extracurricular activities for a week). She then shared that she felt so guilty for not studying and embarrassed for getting caught. She kept apologizing. I told her I was over it, but that she needed to forgive herself because she will make mistakes and bad choices throughout her life, but that it's most important to learn from them and do better. 'When you know better, you do better...' I can't take credit for that gem.

Forgiveness of others: This has its challenges. *One week, KJ was upset by actions and words from both her dad and her stepdad. She was really bent out of shape by the situations and came to talk to me about it. She didn't want to talk to either of them for a very long time. Now, in my house that is something that could never occur. This is your parent, you respect them, and we don't do the silent treatment. I reminded her of these facts. I then shared that her feelings were valid for her and that once things settled down she might want to speak to each of them about her feelings of being hurt by their words.*

She was not feeling that. KJ felt that they were adults and should know that words mean something. She wasn't willing to forgive. I told her that everyone, especially in a heated moment can make a mistake, misspeak, say things that aren't thoughtful, or take a situation out of context. She could either stew in her feelings or attempt to respectfully share them and hope they will do differently in the future.

Forgiving is not forgetting, nor is it saying that the offense is 'okay.' Forgiving is healing for you and the other person. It is saying I value myself and or our relationship too much to let this negativity grow inside of me. We all have this choice. Choose wisely.

Forgiveness from others: Remember me saying you can only control yourself? Well, this is a prime example of that fact. When you have offended or hurt someone, whether intentional or not, seeking forgiveness, especially when it is brought to your attention, can go a long way to mending the situation. All you can do is offer a *sincere* apology. After that, it's up to the person to accept and forgive. I think it is important to note a few things: 1. You can't make anyone accept your apology. 2. Just because you apologize doesn't make their hurt immediately go away. It's up to them to determine how long it will be before they trust you again. 3. Sincere apologies feel different for different people. We'll discuss this more in the next chapter.

When KJ offered an apology to a friend, and she wasn't immediately forgiven, she got an attitude. She felt that her friend should have accepted it and then moved on. I explained that that's not how forgiveness works. That you cannot dictate the apology and the timeline for its acceptance. She needed to drop her attitude and give her friend space to think things over for herself. That all KJ could do was wait for her friend to come around.

Journal Entry:

Chapter 3 – Communication

The exchange of information and news[2]

Effectively communicating with yourself and others is a skill far too many people take for granted. It is good practice to regularly speak positive words to yourself. To let your own body, hear from your own mouth just how special and wonderful it is…you are. Doing this, nurtures your soul, heals your heart, and strengthens your self-esteem and confidence. It also creates a playlist in your head that comes in handy during challenging situations.

We sometimes think that others will think the way we do or will see things from our perspective because it makes perfect sense to us…right? We know this isn't always the case. Therefore, learning how to communicate so your thoughts come across clearly, and that you are listening for understanding and information, rather than to have the right 'come back,' are skills that will help enhance any relationship or interaction you have with someone else.

No one ever really masters communicating effectively all the time. That is because we each are complicated beings with a whirlwind of emotions and energies, at any one given time, trying to connect with another who has their own orbit of emotions and energies whirling. However, we each have a responsibility, to ourselves and those we interact with, to communicate in meaningful and productive ways for positive outcomes.

Speaking Your Mind: Saying firmly and honestly what you think about a situation, even if this may offend or upset people.[21]

"We must teach our girls that if they speak their mind, they can create the world they want to see." -Robyn Silverman

From a fairly young age I let KJ know it was ok to speak her mind. But there were a few rules of engagement she needed to adhere to. Understandably, moving along these fine lines has not always been easy for her, nor for me as her mom. As a budding teenager, KJ was full of opinions.

It's ok to ask the questions "why" or "why not," when given direction, but she could do it when she was being disciplined. She also needed to learn that when being disciplined, she didn't have the right to an answer- sometimes you just have to toe the line because you were told to. I wanted her to learn how to make sound decisions for reasons beyond fear of punishment. I believe my job as a parent to an adolescent was to raise and nurture my child in such a way that as she grew into her own she would naturally move, mentally and physically, into the world as a confident and well-equipped person.

Parents now let me warn you, you may question yourself about developing this quality in your child, especially as they start to feel the intense need to share just what they think about *whatever they feel, whenever they feel it*. But breathe, and firmly remind them that just because they think it, doesn't mean they should say it! That was another frequent saying of mine. It needed to be stated often during her 12th year! (And probably into her 20's!)

There was a situation when KJ's math teacher snatched and threw away a paper from her tutor without asking any questions about it. I had one extremely angry seventh grader who couldn't wait to get home and tell me what happened. This made me equally as angry. I immediately called the school to speak with the teacher. I set up a meeting for the next morning. That evening, still seething, KJ had some clear ideas as to how I should handle the situation, including suggesting that I use colorful words and get in the teacher's face. I told her that 1) she knew that wasn't my style, and 2) if I did behave in that manner, they would immediately call the resource officer to put me out and possibly ban me from the campus. And if that occurred how could I effectively support her in the future.

At the meeting, in which the vice principal and two other teachers attended, KJ was still visibly angry with her leg shaking, tight lips, squinted eyes and fully red face. Although everyone could clearly see the steam coming from her ears, KJ was successful in keeping her words to herself while I handled the situation.

Just in case you were wondering, the meeting ended with an apology from the teacher to Kamaria and an assurance to me, by the vice principal, that this was not something that would ever happen again. While I was satisfied with the outcome KJ still would have preferred that choice words were said.

As the adult she continues to grow into today, she has learned better timing on when and how to speak her mind in advocating for herself and others. She speaks at townhall meetings, handles her business with vendors, and appropriately engages with others, both personally and professionally. It has been worth the time and occasional aggravation to help her develop this skill. Even though there are still times when she'd prefer to use choice words, she typically seeks a sounding board to help determine the best course of action and words to say.

Journal Entry:

Body language: The process of communicating nonverbally through conscious or unconscious gestures and movements.[3]

"The willingness to show up changes us, it makes us a little braver each time." - Brené Brown

How you physically show up in the world matters. Body language is strongly connected to personal appearance, but body language plays a much bigger role. While others may notice what you wear, they will most likely remember how you wore it, how you carried yourself in it. Without speaking a word, your physical presence speaks volumes about you.

Quick check-in quiz:

Do you enter a room confidently or do you look for the closest wall to press up against?

Do you look people, even adults, in the eye when you meet them, or do you lift your eyes briefly then quickly look away?

Do you shake hands firmly or extend a limp hand just giving them fingertips and a soft shake?

Do you feel comfortable in your own skin or feel like everyone can see every hair out of place, or worst yet, every thought swirling in your head, so you try to make yourself invisible by rounding your shoulders, bowing your head, and clasping your hands down in front of you?

At the age of 7, I started teaching Kamaria how to present herself when she meets an adult: look them in the eye (not necessarily appropriately for all cultures), give a slight smile, offer a strong arm and handshake. This lesson came to me after I met a colleague's teenaged son and daughter. While the son was engaging and very present, the daughter gave me a limp noodle of an arm to shake and almost no eye contact. Although I have no idea what had gone on with this outwardly lovely young lady for her to have these mannerisms, it impressed upon me the need to ensure my daughter, and other girls, were intentionally taught how to make their presence known.

Fast forward to her preteen years, KJ, like many teens, went through the stage of awkwardness, clumsiness, and being unsure of almost anything about herself. Around this time, I began strongly impressing upon her to "pay attention" to herself. At times, my daughter could be extremely aloof, almost to the point of dismissing someone. She may have a look, a slight shrug of the shoulder or barely lift her head to acknowledge words spoken to her. I'll tell you prayer was in full effect during these times! Her behaviors were primarily because she didn't know how to interpret or respond to what was being said or done to her. Whether the words or actions were positive or not, she would have this offsetting physical response more often than I care to admit.

No, this did not sit well with me, especially if it was done towards an adult. If there's one thing that would make me go from zero to 1,000 was a disrespectful child, and Lord, don't let it be my child and definitely not towards me! Along with my reminder (and warning) to her that she can think anything she wants, but doesn't have the right always to say it, I added 'take care that certain thoughts don't show up on your face.'

If you do this too often with your friends, you might find yourself alone. If you do it with adults, you will likely find yourself in big trouble with them and your parents! It is about self-awareness and the presence you have when you engage with others. Just like you matter, let others know that they matter by fully being present in the moment with them.

Journal Entry:

Boundaries & Expectations: Personal boundaries are the limits and rules we set for ourselves within relationships. When boundaries are set, there's an expectation that they will be respected, and setting boundaries helps us know what to expect in our relationship.[8]

"Setting boundaries is a way of caring for myself. It doesn't make me mean, selfish, or uncaring (just) because I don't do things your way. I care about me, too." - Christine Morgan

This is a biggie. Many adults struggle with boundaries. The most important responsibility we have is to take care of ourselves. When we do this for our mind, body, and soul, we love ourselves and therefore can love others. Loving yourself is the most selfless thing you can do. You can't give what you don't have. One of the best ways to love and nurture yourself is to know and adhere to your own boundaries.

Life is 100%. I say 20% are the principles you stand on, believe in, and are willing to go toe to toe over. Everything else is in the 80%, which you can either let slide or make mention of your feelings and thoughts about the situation but then move on from.

Your 20% could be bullying, animal cruelty, littering, being talked about by someone you thought to be a friend…you get the picture. Whatever does not sit well inside your core and won't let you rest is typically in your 20%. As budding teens, you work to find and define what makes you who you are. Friends you played with since Pre-K may start to annoy you. Often, you won't know why your 'friend' is acting like 'this.' I have found this conflict to be when you each start to grow into a new stage of self-awareness and 'voice power.' You begin to determine who you are and subconsciously recognize what works for you. Bringing this subconscious recognition to the forefront allows you to set boundaries and have realistic expectations of yourself and others (your voice power).

When someone oversteps your boundaries, you will know because you've already defined them. Then you can best determine how you want to respond or act as a result. *The first thing I asked KJ when this happened to her was "did your friend know this was a boundary or issue for you?" When she responded 'no' I told her that none of us think nor feel the same way about everything. This is even true for siblings growing up in the same house. Therefore, if you valued the friendship, you might want to tell your friend that this is something you don't like and then ask her not to do it again.*

Key things to remember:

- You can't expect people to know how you feel about something unless you tell them.

- You can't make people do anything. You can only control and manage yourself.

Therefore, all you can do is share your feelings and request to not be in the situation again. It's then okay to expect your friend to respect your wishes. But if or when they do not, you have the right to decide how you want the friendship to look from then on. I always encouraged KJ to expect the best from others, but I also told her that you have an informed decision to make if they don't live up to it.

Journal Entry:

Art of An Apology: Expressing regret for something that one has done wrong.[3]

"Sometimes saying I'm sorry is the most difficult thing on earth. But it's the cheapest thing to save the most expensive gift called relationship. -Unknown
"Men are taught to apologize for their weaknesses, women for their strengths." - Lois Wyze

Why is apologizing so hard to do? It's only two simple words, "I apologize." Yet, it can cause a bad situation to go way left. People hesitate to say it and are skeptical to accept it.

When Kamaria was in elementary school, she would quickly insist she was sorry if her behavior warranted punishment. One time I asked her, if she was sorry because she "did it" or because she got caught? Not expecting me to respond with that question, she stumbled over her answer. Truth was she was sorrier that she had gotten caught and had to take the punishment. After she and I had calmed from the situation, I sat her down and told her that saying "sorry" doesn't absolve the behavior or my feelings about it. If she was really "sorry," she should know why. Being the mom I was, and still am, I took it a step further. I told her for the first time, what would become a standing principle for me. I told her "don't be sorry, be different." For me, saying sorry has little meaning if you continue to behave in the same way. For others, a heartfelt, "I'm sorry" is fine.

As she got older, I shared more about the different types of apologies. Some of you want the offender to make it right and take immediate action to impact the current situation. Others want the person to continually apologize until you are convinced that they mean it or so they never forget the pain it caused you (this one can be a very slippery slope to you never healing and reliving the pain). The point I was making to her was that saying "I'm sorry" will not always be accepted. While she can't make anyone accept her apology, her responsibility is to be sincere in however she apologizes. The rest is up to the other person. Also, when an apology is sent her way, I told her to look at the full relationship with the offender and determine their sincerity and move forward from there.

One last thing about "I'm sorry." As females, we tend to take on the responsibility for other people's feels or situations, when we have absolutely nothing to do with it. Saying "I'm sorry" has the tone that I did something to cause another pain or hurt. I learned this at a women's conference, and it changed my life. Once I learned this, I shared it with KJ and other females. If I am personally responsible for an offense I say, "I'm sorry." If someone shares a sad story or experience, like they are sick or a loved one has passed away, I say, "I'm sad to hear that" or "I give you my sympathy." But I no longer take on the responsibility. It may seem like a small thing, but it really is freeing. Try it.

Journal Entry:

Appreciation & Gratitude: The state of being grateful; a feeling of thankfulness or appreciation.[9]

"Gratitude turns what we have into enough." -Unknown

Being appreciative and grateful - for the small things from a passing smile from a stranger to the birthday gift you were dying for - will take you a long way in life. People like to be acknowledged, point blank, and they really like to be recognized for acts of kindness.

There are two characteristics that, when not displayed by children, make steam burst through my ears! The first I mentioned in Chapter 1 – Respect, and the second is Gratitude. Truthfully, I value these characteristics in adults as well. Most parents do the best they can with the resources they have. Aside from monetary things, there are the resources of hugs, wiping tears, praying, listening to drama-filled teenage stories, driving to practices, recitals, and going back and forth to the store for forgotten items for tomorrow's school presentation!

While KJ did not have all she wanted or asked for, she never had a reason to be ungrateful. And the times she behaved or spoke as if she was – punishment was swift and was accompanied by a long lecture! I reminded her that I was only required to feed, clothe, house, and educate her by law. That none of those things had to come with a fancy price tag. But *by love* I was gladly bound to provide above and beyond, which has allowed for her to remember her childhood as having many great experiences.

One incident sticks out in my mind vividly and occurred when KJ was 12. She was always hanging out or spending the night at a friend's house. I did not mind because they were families we had gotten to know and had been to their homes on different occasions. What I did mind was that no one ever seemed to want to come to our home. I would tell KJ she could have friends over, which she would quickly say 'ok' and move to the next topic.

One Friday evening, while driving home, she asked if she could go over a friend's house for the weekend. I finally asked, very intently, why she never had friends over. My wonderful child tells me she likes to go to their homes because they were bigger and newer than ours. I was crushed and upset! No, I was downright mad! 1) I had fond childhood memories having my sister's or my friends in and out of our house and 2) I wanted to be "that house and that mom" where kids could come and hang out.

She got it with both barrels. Starting with, "how dare you?!" Afterall, our home was just as good as anyone else's. It wasn't the biggest nor newest, but it was comfortable, inviting and filled with love. I then informed my child that she could not go over another person's house until she started having friends at our house. Lastly, I told her she should be grateful we even wanted her little friends over in the first place and she needed to appreciate the love and openness of her own home.

By then she was tearing up and we pulled in the driveway. Still hurt and fuming I ordered her out of the car, gave her a list of chores and told her to tell her stepfather that I'd be back in an hour. I then drove to the closest Walmart and walked around until I calmed down. When I returned there was a tear- soaked note at my bedroom door. Kamaria apologized for hurting my feelings and not appreciating the home we created.

Parents *be careful what you ask for (said with a smile). From then on, we had kids, then teens, then college students, to adult friends (when she comes for a visit) hanging at our home and fondly calling me "mom." And she and I love it!*

You will likely not get everything you want, and as you get older you will be grateful you didn't. But appreciating what you already have opens the door to receiving more.

Journal Entry:

Chapter 4 – Friends

A person whom one knows and with whom one has a bond of

mutual affection, typically exclusive of sexual or family relation.[3]

Are you a leader or a follower? There is no wrong answer. It takes both to get anything done. Who do you hang out with? Are they people you'd want us (your parents/grandparents) to meet? Are you 'grandparent' worthy? Do you and your crew encourage each other or tear each other down with negative comments hidden behind jokes. Will a secret stay within your group or do you gossip about one another? These are important questions to ask yourself and to recognize about your circle. I taught KJ that friends are people you choose to participate in your life. You allow them access to your life; they don't have a right to it. Friends become family by your choice alone.

Reputation: the beliefs or opinions that are generally held about someone or something.[3]

"You can tell more about a person by what (she) he says about others than you can about what others say about (her) him." -Audrey Hepburn

When my daughter was in the fifth grade, two new girls moved to the area and to her class. Kamaria befriended them. Somewhere around the third month of school another girl's purse was stolen. A student saw one of the 'new girls' with it. As the investigation began my daughter was named as one who hung out with the 'new girl' often.

Kamaria was called into the principal's office and questioned about what she knew of the incident. I was called afterward, and I remember clearly what the principal said, "I wanted to tell you that Kamaria was just in my office. I needed to find out what she may have known about the situation. Please know that at no time did any of us accuse her nor believe she had any part in the stealing. We have known her since kindergarten, and we know that this is not a part of who she is. Kamaria said the only thing she knew about the situation was what everyone talked about once it happened. We are satisfied that she is telling all she knew."

I was thrilled to hear that KJ's consistent character created a reputation that allowed her to avoid the consequences of guilt by association. This was definitely a teaching moment for Kamaria and a proud moment for me.

The old saying "birds of a feather flock together" isn't always true. Sometimes you find yourself in a group that you thought were about one thing and it turned out they were the total opposite. It is important to know who you are and what you stand for, your values, your boundaries. Then observe those around you and determine if they fit in your life. We will talk more about this in Peer Pressure. Just know that a good reputation takes time to create and a second to destroy.

Journal Entry:

Conflicts & Disagreements: an extended struggle: battle. A clashing disagreement (as between ideas or interests).[10]

"10% of conflicts are due to a difference of opinion, 90% are due to the wrong tone of voice."- Unknown

"My father used to say, 'Don't raise your voice, raise your argument." -Theresa Tartarone

As you grow and mature you may find yourself in more internal or external conflicts. This may come across as being uncomfortable in certain conversations or situations, getting irritated by things that did not bother you before, or having two opposing thoughts and feelings about a topic that you once felt sure about. These are conflicts that arise because you are shaping and reshaping your values and opinions about your life.

This is completely normal and occurs as you have a greater awareness about the world and your place in it. But while it is normal, it can also be very frustrating or even scary as your newly formed ways of looking at the world around you may pull you away from friends who no longer think like you. There is a time and season for everything under the sun. Not all the relationships you have now are meant to stay with you throughout your life. This could seem like another scary thought. But just trust your feelings and know that everything will work out for your good.

On a one-on-one level, because each person has their own perceptions and thoughts about, well… EVERYTHING, you are destined to have conflicts and disagreements with your closest family members and friends at some point. Sometimes it's your fault, sometimes it's not; sometimes you may be the one to apologize, sometimes not; sometimes the reasons will be valid, sometimes not.

The key things to ask yourself are:

Is the conflict or reason behind the conflict worth arguing over?

Has the person whom you are in conflict with, shown this type of behavior before, if so, is it something you want to keep dealing with (you do have a choice)?

When you have the conflict raging inside of you, which part feels the most like you? Which part makes the most sense to follow?

Which will likely end up better for you and the situation?

Kamaria has had her share of disagreements while growing up. One of the things I have passed on to her is to observe people's words and actions. Do they match? Is this the person's consistent behavior? Is the subject at hand in your 20% or your 80%? Everything is not argue-worthy. You can agree to disagree and keep it moving.

Girls tend to have more disagreements than boys. That's probably because we use more words to express ourselves and because we tend to share, oh…just about… EVERYTHING, whether we are asked or not.

Journal Entry:

Bullying: seek to harm, intimidate, or coerce (someone perceived as vulnerable).[3]

"People say sticks and stones may break your bones, but names can never hurt you, but that's not true. Words can hurt. They hurt me. Things were said to me that I still haven't forgotten." -Demi Lovato

I didn't find out until KJ was in her early 20's that she experienced some bullying in middle school. She intentionally kept it from me. When she told me about the bullying, she shared that it was uncomfortable and hurtful. I'd like to believe, because she received positive reinforcement at home and as a part of groups outside of school, Kamaria was able to use that to navigate those tough times. Through our *'12ᵗʰ Year'* talks, I hope I was unknowingly able to address the bullying she was experiencing.

Our specific *'12ᵗʰ Year'* bullying talk centered around her believing in herself and surrounding herself with friends who felt good about themselves, laughed with one another, had good character and who thought and behaved in similar ways to her own. I'm sure I don't need to tell you that traversing middle school within your own mind can be hectic enough, but when you add the thoughts and insecurities of other middle schoolers it can be unnerving!

Its these insecurities that lead your classmates into bullying. So, you must have a force of good around you. You know, people who help make you feel good about yourself and lift you up! It's not that she and her friends, nor you and your friends, won't experience bullying or your own insecurities of some kind. But, if you can stick together through it all, you have a greater chance of making it through the tough times stronger.

Bullies come in all shapes, sizes, and ages. It is key to recognize a person who has bullying behaviors because you will likely come across someone like them at different stages throughout your lifetime. Though you may never know why a person chooses to bully, being able to determine a bully when you meet one helps you to know how to better interact with them and to not accept what they are saying or doing.

While it may seem that bullying is about you, it is about the bully. Typically, bullies have low self-esteem. Therefore, they bully to make themselves seem more important, better, or more popular than they are.

Do not accept being bullied. Talk to someone you trust, who will support you, and or who can address the situation to correct it (like a parent, teacher or administrator). Bullies continue to bully because no one speaks up. And if you witness bullying, don't stay silent.

Journal Entry:

Peer Pressure: influence from members of one's peer group.[3]

"I've learned that people will forget what you said, people will forget what you did, but people will never forget how you made them feel." -Maya Angelou

"It's better to walk alone than in a crowd going in the wrong direction. Do what you feel is right." -Unknown

Ahhhh, the big elephant in the room for kids from age 4 to…well, adulthood, if we are honest! Whether introverts or extroverts, we are all social beings and are not immune to influences and suggestions. As your parents, some of us have come through the negative experiences of peer pressure unscathed and others of us were caught up, suffered the consequences and are thankfully here to tell the lessons we learned. And that, right there, is the point and purpose of these talks. I am here to teach the lessons I learned so your life journeys will be less bumpy.

Okay, so exactly how can you combat peer pressure? I'm glad you asked! It's very important for you to know that peer pressure is real. You will experience it, and even when you don't think you can, you can always talk to us because we are here for you. These talks will hopefully give you a basis in which you can be grounded in the positives of who you are.

Because KJ was an only child (at least in my house) it was important for me (more than for her) to have a set of friends who could come and go over each other's houses to just hang out. These were girls from school, church, Girl Scouts, and the neighborhood. I would host sleepovers, take them out to eat and to the store, or just let them be. This allowed me to observe and listen to what type of friends KJ had and was attracting, as well as how they played together, and how they worked out conflicts.

Those who exhibited characteristics that were not to my liking I would use these interactions, as teachable moments, in later conversations with KJ. I never called out a friend, nor barred them from our home (unless they refused to follow the same house rules as KJ- thankfully, it never got to that point). What I would do was remind KJ before they came over, that it was her job to make sure her friends knew and followed the house rules. I would step in as necessary to smooth an escalating situation and keep mental notes of behaviors or characteristics I might need to pay more attention to in the future in my daughter, as well as her friends.

When KJ was in the 5ᵗʰ grade she had one of her infamous birthday sleepovers. One of her new school friends was invited along with about six other friends from school and Scouts. The girls were in her room doing girl things and then decided they were hungry. Everyone came down except for the new girl. I pulled KJ to the side and asked where she was, she responded 'sitting in my closet.' Of course, this led to more questions.

Basically, everyone was sitting in the closet making beaded jewelry and having fun. Then one of the girls with a strong personality decided to ask everyone to tell what they liked and didn't like about each other. Everyone was all smiles until the girl who started this wonderful game shared that she really didn't like how the new girl talked. She asked the others what they thought (peer pressure in its most subtle form). One by one, including my precious jewel felt the need to chime in with comments like "it's ok, but yeah kinda annoying," or "I don't really like it, I guess." I had heard enough.

Keeping my calm, I informed KJ that it was her job to ensure that everyone felt included, no one was picked on, and that the house rules were followed. And no rule stated, leave a friend in the closet alone! I told her to take all of her friends back upstairs, be kind, make it right and invite her to eat with them.

Parents, our tweens and teens need to have friends. Some a couple of years younger, some the same age, and some a couple of years older who are like-minded and who have parents who are raising them with similar values that you are instilling in your child. Ultimately, you want the peers to bring out the best in each other. Creating this type of peer environment for your child when she is younger aids in setting a firm foundation that is hard to stray too far away from. If they do stray it's easy to find their way back to. "Train up a child in the way (s)he should go and when (s)he is old, (s)he will not depart from it. (Prov. 22:6)" No matter your religious affiliations or beliefs, this is wisdom, plain and simple. Learn about "The Girlfriends' Club" at the end of the book. It's an idea I had, along with other mothers to create such an environment of peers for our girls.

Journal Entry:

Competition: strive to gain or win something by defeating or establishing superiority over others who are trying to do the same.[3]

"The flower does not think of competing to the flower next to it, it just blooms." - Zen Shin

When Kamaria was around 8 I asked her if she would like to take tennis lessons. She said yes, so I signed her up. KJ has a raw athletic ability so I thought tennis would be good to help her focus, make some new friends, learn a new sport and skill, and expend some excess energy. What I had not yet realized about my daughter was that she had a bit of perfectionism in her.

She would be really hard on herself if she didn't do as well as the other students in her group lesson. She was also hard on herself if she didn't learn a new skill almost immediately. There were two things I had to impress upon her: 1) was that everyone had their own skill abilities, and some had playing tennis for a little longer than she had, so she should not try to compare herself with any of them. Just do her best. 2) was that while she is only supposed to compete against herself, it was called tennis lessons for a reason. She is not supposed to nor expected to be a pro. She is learning the game and its basics. That the goal in any class is for her to improve over time. This was a reoccurring theme as KJ joined middle school teams. She was extraordinarily hard on herself if she did not grasp something immediately.

As my friend, author Wil Dieck says, *"everyone starts at the beginning."* While you may not be the strongest softball batter, the fastest runner, or first to finish your test, the objective is to start. Then continue practicing, learning, and getting better than you were when you first started.

There can be competition amongst members in any team activity or sports to become captain, prima ballerina, or first chair. Though there is only one top spot everyone on the team has to do their specific part to in order for the team to be a good team and be successful. You win together, you lose together.

Compete against yourself. Be better than you were 10 minutes or two hours ago; better than you were yesterday. Pick an area of your life and work on you. Remember, you can only control you, let them' worry about themselves.

Journal Entry:

Chapter 5 – Your Purpose – Your Destiny

Destiny is a condition foreordained by Divine or human will.

Purpose is the reason a person was created.[23]

I could talk about purpose, destiny, and the future all day, every day with Kamaria, with anyone. It is the endless quest we all take. I say it is endless because we are always growing, seeking, evolving into better versions of ourselves. Therefore, when we accomplish one goal, we are not supposed to stop, we move on to the next. And the next. And the next…

Once you were able to hold a real conversation, one of the questions you were asked was, "what do you want to be when you grow up?" We all were asked this same question. And that's when the quest began.

Most parents want the best for each of our children. We try to shape your interests, guide you in a certain direction, even tell you what we believe you are or want you to do and be. Sometimes our guidance is subtle, other times overt, pushy, and demanding. Truth is, we each must find and follow our own paths. This journey is not always easy and very seldom is it straight forward. Most times it comes with detours, U-turns, and seemingly more questions than we have the immediate answers for. BUT it is ALWAYS WORTH taking!

Future Planning & Goal Setting: Goal setting is the process of deciding what you want to accomplish and devising a plan to achieve those desired results.[11]

"Dance. Smile. Giggle. Marvel. TRUST. HOPE. LOVE. WISH. BELIEVE. Most of all, enjoy every moment of the journey, and appreciate where you are at this moment instead of always focusing on how far you have to go." -Mandy Hale

Goals are dreams, desires, hopes, and plans that you wish to achieve at some point in the future. And the future could be a day, a year or a decade. I don't know any child who doesn't or hasn't confessed their fabulously huge plan for their future. And I encourage you to share your biggest plan with at least one trusted and supportive family member or friend. If there is no living being you feel safe to share your goals with, tell your pet, favorite stuffed animal, or write it down and anonymously leave it on a favorite teacher's desk. It doesn't matter how wild or far-reaching your goal may seem. Shout it from the rooftops and declare it in the atmosphere! Get your goal out of you. Give it air and room to grow. The point is to dream. And dream BIG.

"No one is you, and that is your Superpower." -Elyse Santilli

"Little girls with dreams, become women with vision." -Unknown

"Be the girl who turned her cant's into cans, and her dreams into plans." - Unknown

Set your intention. Research what you want your future to look like. What will it take to get there? Are there any certifications, degrees, or internships you need to have? Who is doing what you want to do? Once you figure that out start researching the person. How did they start? How did they fail? Wait, FAIL?!...That's right, fail. In our failing we learn what not to do the next time! How did they grow? Take the risk, reach out to them, and ask questions.

"The person I am today would like to thank the person I was five years ago for not giving up. You're awesome!" -Iva Ursano

In elementary school, KJ declared she wanted to be a veterinarian. Of course, I was thrilled, I'd have a daughter who was a doctor! She talked about it all the time. I got her age-appropriate books, we learned how to care for horses, and she learned how to care after her own pet – Hopper, her long-eared rabbit. When she was 12, I convinced Hopper's vet to let KJ volunteer a couple of hours a week in his clinic. She would help walk the dogs, sit with them when she thought they looked homesick, and feed them. We were all thrilled. KJ even had a junior vet kit which she used to practice her skills on Hopper at home. Sadly, Hopper was diagnosed with tumor, and had to be put to sleep. Kamaria asked to hold him while he was going to sleep. The vet and I agreed this would be helpful for her.

The whole situation made her incredibly sad and ultimately changed her mind about becoming a veterinarian. That apparently, wasn't her destiny. But now, while I don't have a daughter who is a doctor, I am very proud of the awesome businesswoman she has become!

"I don't like to gamble, but if there's one thing I'm willing to bet on, it's myself." - Beyonce

Again, determine what goals and dreams you have. Really visualize yourself in the future doing whatever it is you believe you were created for. Then share that desire, first with the universe and then with someone trusted. This is like planting a seed in the ground. Next, do your homework gather the what's, whys, where's, when's, and how's of your future. This is nurturing, watering, and feeding your seed.

Now, act. What is one thing you can do using the information you have collected to move toward your goal? Read an article, watch a video, contact someone who is already doing it? You get the idea. With each action you will see your seed grow and blossom. This is goal setting, planning, and implementation. Once you gain this skill you can use it to act on any goal you set for yourself throughout your life. This is how dreams become reality.

"The most difficult thing is the decision to act. The rest if merely tenacity." -Amelia Earhart

One word of insight: As you grow and develop, your goal, dream or vision of your future self may change. And that's not a bad thing. We are living beings who shift and evolve over time. Just know that this may happen, but don't beat yourself up about it. Go with the flow of your true self and start setting, planning, and implementing that new goal! You will find that women are great at reinventing ourselves!

"There is nothing stronger than a broken woman who has rebuilt herself." - Hannah Godsby

Journal Entry:

Education: an enlightening experience.[3]

"Believe in yourself, learn, and never stop wanting to build a better world." -Mary McLeod Bethune

As long as we are alive, we are meant to learn. This is how we can grow into the better versions of ourselves. This is how we gain better understanding of ourselves, our family and friends, and the world around us. Now, education is not just what you learn in school and textbooks. Life gives each of us a lesson or two every day. We need to be open to the knowledge and use it in ways that help ourselves and others.

While you are in school, understanding your subject matter is your number one job. Hanging with your friends, going to sporting events, being on teams are important, but learning comes first. Simply put, if you don't learn your lessons, you will fail your tests. If you fail too many tests, you won't pass the class. If you fail too many classes, you will be held back. If you are held back to many times, you will likely drop out and thereby miss hanging with your friends, going to sporting events or being on a team. See how that works?!

Something that most preteens and teens say is, "I can't wait to grow up. Leave the house. Live by my own rules and make my own money!" Usually said with some kind of smart mouth. And depending on the house you are growing up in, you probably say it under your breath, and behind a closed door soft enough that your parent can't hear it! Kamaria was growing up in *that* kind of house.

Of course, Kamaria had her, "I can't wait until I'm grown and making money" comments. They just didn't come with through a smart mouth. Around 10 or 11 I started having KJ filling out checks for me (your parents will explain what checks are or were...smh!), everything but the signature. It was mostly out of convenience because I was doing something else. But I thought it was good for her to learn how to complete them (who knew it wouldn't be relevant a few decades later), and I wanted her to see the real cost and responsibility of being 'grown and making your own money.' She learned that being 'grown' isn't the constant fun and games she thought.

As Mr. Julius, a grumpy old man I knew when I was a teenager, would say, "childhood is wasted on the young!" I thought it was the most ridiculous thing I ever heard, until I became an adult. I shared his words with KJ when we discussed her education. What Mr. Julius meant was that as kids we can't wait to grow up and therefore overlook the joyous freedoms that come with being a kid.

What you can't see, is that childhood: being free to play and be silly, only having to do homework and some chores, having someone buy food and cook for you, and be responsible for your clothes and other major needs is such a short period of hopefully your long life. Once you are 'grown' bills come in your name every month. And depending on your financial situation if you don't work you don't eat. Therefore, you must make decisions now for your life that you will live in in the future.

So, getting your education helps with making those 'grown' decisions. Getting a quality education in which, you are paying attention, understanding the material, asking questions, getting help and passing tests with good grades helps to determine your future financial situation based on the career options you have. Your education isn't free. It costs your time, effort, and energy. It may sometimes cost you some sleep. But the benefits and freedoms that come with school age education will be appreciated by you when you are 'grown' and taking the world by storm!

Journal Entry:

Careers - Your Life's Work: an occupation undertaken for a significant period of a person's life and with opportunities for progress.[3]

"Don't sit down and wait for opportunities to come. Get up and make them." -
Madam C.J. Walker

This is intricately connected to our talk on goal setting and planning. However, the focus here is on living towards your dream while being open to the dream changing. We all are blessed with many different talents and interests. We don't have one dream. We may not have one career. Dream and *Dream Big*. Never stop dreaming.

Never stop learning new things about yourself and the world. I can't tell you how many dreams, goals, and career ideas have passed through Kamaria, starting at a young age. I encouraged her to explore all of them. While we have family businesses, KJ's career path did not lead her in those directions. And that's ok. The planning process is a creative process. And creativity breeds more creativity. Your thoughts today may lead you to another thought that ends up being the career you were born to do.

You may have skills that you don't necessarily recognize or may not want to accept, but others take note and tell you how good you are or could be at this or that. Much to my feeble resistance, my mini-me grew taller than me starting at age 10 (FYI-we both are standing in the pic on the back cover).

Because of her long legs and appearance, people used to say she should, or ask if she did, play basketball or model. KJ would get so annoyed by these comments or questions. I would tell her that those were natural conclusion for many to associate with her. I asked why she got upset since she used to play basketball when she was a little younger and has never modeled. She really didn't have an answer. At 12 she took up basketball again for a couple of years, and when she was in high school, she started modeling – go figure! Don't be so quick to dismiss what qualities and skills others notice about you. They may be worth exploring down the road.

Because of my experiences, I wanted to make sure KJ understood that our plans and dreams may change or never happen. I believe it is important to acknowledge that life may take you down roads you had not imagined. The goal you have been dreaming about since you were a little girl may, out of nowhere, be dead before it begins.

I shared with KJ some of my plans that never materialized or ways I got sidetracked by life events. Sometimes I could control them and sometimes I couldn't. So, to her, and now to you, I say be open to the unexpected opportunity, the random thought that can shift your focus, the spark that you didn't know you had for something to rise in you, and the disappointment that could lead to fulfillment.

It's important not to box yourself in, especially while you are young. Let me correct that...don't box yourself in at any age. The same research you did when goal setting, do that for each new possibility. You may not get as deep with it, but then again, maybe you are so intrigued that you naturally become lost in it for hours. This is not a bad thing. What gets your heart beating at 12 may or may not be what keeps it beating at 18 or 24 or 35 (yeah, I know 35 sounds really old – but trust me, it's not!).

Just know, throughout your life you will reinvent yourself – out of necessity or want. Be okay with that. Kamaria became good at investigating her interests and sharing them with me. Some were funny, some deep, and some made me raise my eyebrows.

In today's virtual society, we can see people living fabulous lives. We often only see their end result while not seeing the journey of challenges, obstacles, stops and starts, failures and sweat it took for them to get to and maintain *fabulous* (many times their fabulous is not as fabulous as it *looks*). Don't compare your life with anyone else's.

"Follow your path and be mindful of the cracks in sidewalks – a beautiful flower just may spring from below." -Dr. Lisa

Journal Entry:

Chapter 6 – Dating

Dating is where two people who are attracted to each other

spend time together to see if they also can stand to be around

each other most of the time…[12]

Well, here we go! Another big elephant in the room that makes many parents anxious and young girls excited. The fact of the matter is, we need to have 'the talk' with you before you start talking with your peers. It's more important for you to know you can come to us, ask real questions and get solid answers. And sometimes, I said SOMEtimes, *'I don't know'* and *'we will talk about that at another time'* are valid answers about relationships. I will admit the conversations are not always easy nor comfortable for us as parents or you say children. But they can reap great rewards down the road to increase respect, honest communication, and bonding in our relationships. And these talks have also saved lives from violence in dating relationships and other things we don't want you to experience.

Dating is the ultimate practice for sharing your best self, receiving the best from someone else, setting healthy boundaries, and making decisions for how others treat you. Up until now, you have had only your family and friends to share your heart. There are special feelings, your heart's desires, that you will want to share with that one special person in dating. That is natural. That is special. That is to be honored and not taken advantage of. As KJ sat trying her best not to make eye contact with me during most of the talks below, I would say, *"let's jump in with both feet!"* I sounded confident, but my knees were shaking, and I was silently praying!

Falling in Love: The moment when you pass from a state of being friends with a person to loving them in a romantic way.[4]

"Love is a commitment to care." -Darlene Sala

Love is wonderful! Love is fun! Exciting! Magical! Love is a commitment. It's a conscious and intentional decision to put someone else's cares above our own. But, LET ME BE CLEAR... putting someone else before ourselves doesn't mean we do it if it will cause us physical, mental, or emotional harm! We are to love ourselves first.

Most of us never forget our first love. Some may call it puppy love. But for the two people involved its real. I experienced it, your dad and grandparents did too, all of us have. Each time we fall in love, we are supposed to grow from the lessons we have already learned. We are to be a better version of ourselves. Love should be an intentional decision.

Love gives. Love is an action word. Love makes us strive to give the best to ourselves and to the one we love.

When Kamaria was 14, she experienced her first crush, at least it was the first I knew about. She was not allowed to date yet, but age doesn't stop the heart from feeling what it feels. She and the boy were allowed to talk on the phone in group conversations, with other friends. As KJ would talk to me about him, I could see her eyes light up. She asked if we would consider moving her dating age, because she was sure she was ready. We did not. But I told her this was a time for her to figure out what she liked about this boy. I then asked her a few questions for her consideration:

"What qualities he had that made her feel like he would be a good boyfriend?"

"What qualities did she have that would make her a good girlfriend? "

"What did she think dating is supposed to be about?"

Of course, she really wasn't interested in having a conversation at that time. She simply wanted me to say "yes, you can date." But, once she started to show interest in dating, I knew it was my time to help shape her thoughts and direct future conversations.

I let KJ know that as fun and wonderful as love can be, love can and will break your heart at some point (or points) in your life! This is because we fall in love with other people, and no one is perfect. That is why you have to pay attention to who you love and how they love you back. Their walk should match their talk. Love shouldn't be secret. Love shouldn't hurt. Love disappoints, and disappointment hurts. Your heart will ache. But you will love again.

Journal Entry:

Mercy #s & Mercy Dates: When you give out your number or go on a date solely because you feel bad for the other person or you don't want to seem mean, you haven't had a date in a long time, or some other reason other than genuinely being interested in that person, then it's not worth it. (Original definition)

"Do what your heart tells you to do." -Princess Diana

After sharing my own experiences of going on mercy dates, I will explain my full list of reasons why they aren't a good idea: it's starting a relationship on a lie, its selfish, people get hurt, it's a waste of your time and their time, the hurt person may seek revenge, it could lead to unhealthy relationship situations and habits, and worse of all, it can lead to dating violence.

As you have figured, Kamaria and I talked a lot. Or should I say, I talked a lot to her. I wanted her to learn lessons from my mistakes so that she would not have to travel up the hilly and rocky roads I traveled. And boy was 'mercy dating' or 'number giving' a rough road for me! I believe I shared my stories with KJ so clearly that she was too afraid to do it. So, I don't have a story of hers to share. But I would encourage you to ask your parents, who were once believe it or not young dating people, to share their story related to mercy numbers or dating. Your parents may share their real stories and the lessons learned. This will provide you with the necessary tools to hopefully avoid these pitfalls.

Parents be open to sharing your stories. If you are not, check-in with why you might not be willing to share your story with your child. While not all story details may be appropriate, the lessons may be helpful to your child, in the future. I will continue to say, knowledge is power. Empower your child to make wise dating choices from the lessons you may have learned the hard way.

Journal Entry:

Dating Older Guys: Spending time with a guy who is at least two years older with the purpose of getting to know each him romantically (original definition).

"Once you date a guy a couple of years older than yourself, guys your own age look young and stupid." -Meghan Scott

Though you both are still considered teenagers, the development and focus are almost completely different when there's even a two-year age gap. Therefore, my dating rule is the same age or one year difference.

Most parents set an age when our daughters can start dating. Often that age is around 15 or 16. KJ's age was 15. Like KJ, most of you start thinking about dating way before then, so this topic needs to be discussed before then.

Between 13 and 15 years old, KJ participated in a two-week Summer arts program at a university about two hours away from home. We both looked forward to it. For me, I loved the beautiful scenic drive through the country. As well as the two-week 'child-free' time I was about to have. For Kamaria, she got to stay on a college campus with new people doing things she enjoyed and having a 'parent-free' vacay (Let's keep it real)!

At the end of camp her last summer, there was a boy who caught her attention. He was entering his senior year and she her sophomore year, and somewhere near the middle of the school year, they decided to date. Now, KJ knew my rule about the two-year difference, but thought she knew better. At first, I did not approve, but I decided - against my better judgment- to let them 'talk." He lived in the town where the summer program was held. I thought, he was safe since they would not get to see one another unless I decided to take a country drive. Like I said, I acted against my better judgment.

Aside from me occasionally taking her phone, so she could take care of her responsibilities (chores and homework) they were content, and I was content. Then came his last months of high school, and the summer. Let's go back to how I started this section...the focus being completely different with the age differences. The once content relationship started to get strained. He was always hanging with his friends, talking about college, being 'soooo' ready to leave...while Kamaria was focused on their next phone call and wondering how they could see each other. The emotions, the tears, the little arguments, and misunderstandings began. How could he really love me and be so excited about leaving me?

Then came his first two months of college (within the state, but about three and a half hours away, still safe). The calls or the reliability of him calling when he said become rare. He had to study, he had class, he was working, he was sleeping, he was practicing...while KJ was waiting and waiting for her phone to ring.

I reminded her of my two-year rule. I explained it to her like this: You are at the playground, the same playground you have enjoyed for years. There is nothing new and exciting, it's fun, but its routine. He, well, he just got a free pass to Disneyland for the first time. There is so much to see, new faces, new foods, and exciting rides. Oh, and it's an unlimited pass, he can enjoy it for as long as he wants. It's not that he doesn't love or care about you, it's the natural order. And when you graduate and get to college you will understand exactly what I mean.

He broke her heart by ending the relationship. After that, she either dated within her age or one year older. Of course, this didn't soothe her hurting heart at the time, but when her freshman year of college came, she completely understood.

Journal Entry:

Abuse: Any action that intentionally harms or injures another person.[13]

"The most common way people give up their power is by thinking they don't have any." -Alice Walker

According to www.TheHotLine.org, in one year, 1 in 10 high school students reported having experienced violence at the hands of an intimate partner. That is 1 in 10 too many! The Healthy Relationship 101 - Teen Dating Violence Awareness! Curriculum breaks it down: 1 in 11 female teens and 1 in 15 teen boys will experience physical dating violence. ny.gov reports, "62% of tweens say they know friends who have been verbally abused: called stupid, worthless, ugly, etc. by a boyfriend or girlfriend." This can't be ignored.

Emotional abuse: and mental abuse involves a person acting in a way to control, isolate, or scare somebody else. The form of abuse may be statements, threats, or actions, and there may be a pattern or regularity to the behavior.[30] Emotional abuse can involve any of the following: Verbal abuse: yelling at you, insulting you or swearing at you. Rejection: Constantly rejecting your thoughts, ideas and opinions. Gaslighting: making you doubt your own feelings and thoughts, and even your sanity, by manipulating the truth.[23]

Physical abuse: is Using or threatening to use physically assaultive behaviors such as hitting, shoving, grabbing, slapping, beating, kicking, etc.[31]

Now, read each of those definitions again.

Parent, dating may be a few years away for your daughter. But this book is about conversation starters. It's important for her healthy development to have these talks. She needs to know that she has a trusted parent or parent-figure she can talk to about, well, anything! She needs to understand these truths before she starts dating. It will help her begin recognizing potential warning signs and taking the appropriate steps to end an abusive relationship before it even has a chance to begin!

Kamaria knew she deserved the best. That's because I regularly reminded her of that fact. The best you deserve begins with you treating yourself with love, respect, care, and compassion. It begins with knowing that YOU ARE ENOUGH (see the poem in Appendix A)! We each have flaws and areas we need to improve upon and grow in. That's the common nature of life. Nothing is perfect. You are a work in progress. That's the first thing to recognize and acknowledge.

The next thing is to learn you show others how to treat you by how they see you treat yourself. I told KJ that we would revisit this topic at varying times in the future. I wanted to reinforce that I was here for her and not to accept mistreatment of any kind. Don't settle for someone else's definition of who you are, know within yourself that you are worthy of a healthy relationship. There is someone loving, caring, respectful and kind who will discover just how loving, caring, respectful and kind you are, and who will be worthy of your time, attention, and affection.

"The most beautiful thing you can wear is your confidence." -Blake Lively

I shared with Kamaria my story of an abusive relationship that I found myself in during high school. Truth is the relationship started by me going on a few "mercy dates" with a guy that resulted in date rape. When I was growing up, there wasn't a term for what happened. I just believed it was my own stupidity, and because it was my first sexual experience, I thought I needed to stay in the relationship. I was in it for a year. No one knew about it until I was an adult. Creating a safe space for Kamaria to have this kind of difficult conversations was a priority for me. Thankfully, I do not have story to share regarding Kamaria and dating abuse. Hopefully, you won't have one either.

Journal Entry:

Chapter 7 – Sex

Sexual activity, including specifically sexual intercourse.[3]

"Intimacy is not a purely physical. It's the act of connecting with someone so deeply, you feel like you can see into their soul." -Unknown

Because of the sensitive nature in this chapter, it is written a bit differently than the rest. It is written primarily to parents.

This is the most shied away from topic between parents and children. But in proper perspective, it shouldn't be. It is a natural part of each of our developmental processes, it is a "coming of age" for our children. After all, one day in the future (distant future, that is) most of us hope to become grandparents! But it is this "coming of age" that many parents have difficulty with, because our babies are no longer babies. This topic may bring up painful memories of our own early sexual experiences. We may be embarrassed even to say the word 'sex,' or we may think that talking about 'it' will encourage our children to engage in 'it.'

The difficulty or challenge for many of our children is three-fold: 'how can I actually talk to my parent about this ultra-personal subject? They won't understand what I am feeling,' or 'they might think I want to have sex right now, when I just want to make sense of all of this,' or the realization may hit them that their own parents had sex (far too horrible to even imagine)!

KJ was no different. But she knew, no matter the thoughts, apprehensions, or concerns the conversations were going to be had. I told her, "you will either start having them with your friends, with the person you are interested in or the person who is pressuring you to have sex even though you aren't ready or interested. You may have the talk through social media or in chat groups. But you will have the conversation with me. It will be fact-filled, open and honest."

Much to their possible outward resistance, our children want to know, that no matter the subject, they can turn to us and will get straight answers. Don't we want to provide the needed and desired information about sex in an age-appropriate way to our children? Do we want to be the safe and trusted place for our children to bring their smallest and largest cares, concerns, and challenges?

Some may answer, "No." And that's your right. However, I would encourage you to consider why you answered no, just for your own self-discovery. I did not have these types of conversations with my parents. They never opened a real door for the subject, and I didn't know it was something I should talk with them. I am glad that Spirit led me to have them with my daughter. In hindsight, she is too!

Whether you, as the parent, answered "yes" or "no," It is my hope that this chapter will provide guidance, courage, insight or talking points for healthy, sometimes funny, possibly stutter-filled, and meaningful conversations in your home, the car or in the park. Now, take a deep breath and *"let's jump in with both feet."*

Intercourse: Physical sexual contact between individuals that involves the genitalia.[10]

"Sex is an act of love, not the definition of love." -Unknown

Intercourse is the physical inner-action of people the includes at least one person's genital parts. That's the straight-forward physicality of it all. But so much more goes into the act and can come from the act. Sexual intercourse is supposed to be about the intimacy of two people who are willingly and lovingly committed to one another.

Intimacy: In-to-me-see. It is the giving of one's body to another to be cared for and loved in a way no one else could. While it is physical, it is deeply spiritual and emotional. You leave a part of yourself with that person and they leave a part of themselves with you. As a result of the sex act. It is a decision each party should make individually. It is an action you should only take after intentional thought and recognition of your own physical, emotional, and spiritual readiness. When occurring at the right time, it is a wonderful thing. But don't be fooled, sex is very heavy stuff.

When KJ was 12, we had the first of many chats, discussions, and lectures about sex. Like I've said before, they weren't always easy nor pretty, but they were necessary. Often, I would just listen to her thoughts to see where her head was or see what she was hearing from her friends. Listening was difficult, but insightful.

I had been reading the book, "Power of a Praying Parent" by Stormie O'Martin. In it she talks about asking God to show you when something is going on with your child and how to best address it. Well, one day, God definitely showed me that I needed to talk with KJ. When she was a much older teenager, she was hanging out with her boyfriend and his family for a few hours on a Saturday. This was nothing new, but I felt I needed to pick her up early so we could talk. After scoping her up and driving to the park, I simply asked her if there was something she needed to talk about. A bit uneasy and curious as to my actions, she first responded, 'no.' I told her God was letting me know that we needed to talk, and I couldn't shake the feeling.

We walked quietly for a moment, then she plopped on a nearby bench with face in hands crying and apologizing. This was her first sexual act and it was mutually agreed upon, as she thought she was ready. But she wasn't. She started crying so they immediately stopped. We talked, I reminded her that while she was physically ready, she wasn't emotionally nor mentally ready. We later went to the doctor to have her examined. She and the young man continued to date, just under very watchful eyes. Oh, I also had a conversation with him as well. One thing I told him was I appreciated that he cared enough about her to stop when he saw her crying.

Journal Entry

Oral Sex: Sexual activity in which the genitals of one partner are stimulated by the mouth of the other. [3]

"I am not afraid of the storms for I am learning how to sail my ship." -Louisa May Alcott

First let me say, I do not go into any details about the acts. This is taboo in many cultures, and I respect that. It can also be an unimaginable conversation for us to have with our children, no matter their age. BUT, far too many elementary (YES, I said elementary), middle and high school students don't think oral sex as sex nor as being potentially harmful. And that is why, no matter our beliefs, I believe it should be addressed. Knowledge is power. If our children are armed with the right knowledge, they can make the best decision and know if or when they need to tell a trusted adult if something is going on.

Here are the facts:

- I had this extremely uncomfortable, for both of us, conversation with KJ telling her what the acts entailed.

- I stuttered my way through.

- She was thoroughly disgusted and in disbelief that people would think to do this.

- She learned that it is considered a sexual act.

- She learned that diseases could spread through it.

- And most importantly, she learned that YOU DON'T EVER OWE it to anyone to perform or allow them to perform this.

Journal Entry:

LGBTQ: An acronym for lesbian, gay, bisexual, transgender, and queer or questioning. These terms are used to describe a person's sexual orientation or gender.[14]

"Be proud to be you." -Tyra Banks

While members of the LGBTQ community, for the most part, are no longer in the closet hiding their sexual orientations, there are those who still struggle internally and are persecuted externally for how they identify. I am not here to condemn. I am here to share how I approached the conversation with my 12-year daughter in hopes that it will help other parents in their conversations.

As KJ was doing her homework at the kitchen table, while I cooked dinner, I asked her how she might approach the following scenario: "Let's say you were really upset and crying to one of your good, good girlfriends about something your boyfriend had done. She knows all of your thoughts and secrets. You two are just that close. As you have your head on her shoulder for comfort, something you both have naturally given each other since you were little, she does something new. She leans in and kisses you on the lips. You pull back in surprise. How would you handle the situation?"

At first KJ said, "Mom, that would never happen. I know my friends and none of them are gay." I then said, "just suppose it happened, what would you do?" She then responded, "I'd first stop crying and ask her what she did that for. Then, I'd tell her don't do it again." I said, "ok." Then I went on to share that some young people aren't sure, some are embarrassed, and others may just want to experiment. Whatever their orientation was, that it was important for KJ to know who she was.

KJ assured me that she liked boys. I assured her that I would always love her no matter what and she could share anything with me, whether I wanted to hear it or not, even if it took her an hour to get the words out.

Journal Entry:

Harassment & Unwanted Advances: Harassment can include "sexual harassment" or unwelcome sexual advances, requests for sexual favors, and other verbal or physical harassment of a sexual nature. Harassment does not have to be of a sexual nature, however, and can include offensive remarks about a person's sex.[15]

"We need a world where women don't get sexually harassed. Full stop. Period." - Sheryl Sandberg

Maybe I should have titled this chapter "Knowledge is Power." Again, when you know how to recognize a 'thing' you are better equipped to deal with it. It's important to pay attention to our children's cues when it comes to intimate interactions with older children and adults.

Often, we make our children give other adults, family and family friends, hugs and kisses out of respect and love. When our children are hesitant to do so we tell them not to be 'shy,' 'rude' or 'funny acting.' Nine times out of 10 our children may just not feel like being bothered, are cranky, or don't like the way the person smells or squeezes them so tight. But then there's that one time that just may be the sign that something is very wrong. I believe it is important to have conversations with our children early about *their* comfort levels with *their* personal space. As adults we don't want to be forced into sharing our space and neither should we force our children. It's a talk that should be had in age-appropriate ways and at different developmental stages in their lives.

I was a member of a particular group from when my daughter was born until she was in middle school. One day after rehearsal, when KJ was about 4, she and one of the group members hugged goodbye as always, but this time he gave her a quick peck on the lips. I directly and firmly addressed his action, telling him not to do that again.

Without making a bid deal, I later showed her how to politely turn her head if it looked like an adult male or female was about to kiss her on her lips. That was not to say that this act can be, or in this case wasn't, perfectly innocent, nor to disparage this act of genuine love in anyone else's family. This is just something we do not do in our family, and I needed to set those boundaries.

I remember one summer we were out shopping, Kamaria was around 14 and had nothing but long legs extending from her shorts. While I was looking at some items, I felt her back press up against me and then she grabbed and squeezed my hand in a way that made me stop what I was doing.

When I looked at her, she had a strange look on her face. She then said that an older man was staring at her and smiling. That she felt creepy. Of course, I immediately turned to find out what was going on. Sure enough, there was a much older man who quickly turned away. Now, I won't go into the details of the words he FELT from me regarding his disgusting and highly inappropriate behavior toward my 14-year-old. But let's just say he wasn't the only one who heard, and I wasn't the only one looking at him as he immediately rushed out of the store.

I assured KJ that only he was completely in the wrong for the way he was looking at her. I thanked her for letting me know what was happening so that I could protect her. I reminded her that she could also come to us if and whenever she felt uncomfortable about how someone looked at, spoke to, or touched her.

Harassers will only stop if they are called out for their behaviors. So, I always encouraged KJ to speak up if or whenever she felt she was being targeted by such actions. Your voice is your power!

Journal Entry:

Pornography: Printed or v
display of sexual organs or activit₎
or emotional feelings.[3]

"Your body is a temple, but only if you t₎

   This is another topic I will keep very high lₑ
I discussed pornography, it was also accompanied ₍
lot more information is openly discussed about sex sl₎
and ways to prevent and subvert these things from happ
was still so much that was quietly accepted, and disconneₑ   ₎es.
Human trafficking seemed like something that only happenₑ   ₎ures or
countries outside of the U.S.

   Part of our discussion was a reminder about physical safety, knowing your
surroundings, being where you were supposed to be and with whom you were supposed
to be. You never know when your dad or I may come by for whatever reason. You never
know who we know, who knows you, or may be out where you are, so make sure you are
doing what you are supposed to be doing and taking care when you do it. Though you
may think I am being overprotective or a helicopter parent, you are the only you I have.
It is my job to keep you safe to the best of my abilities. I have no apologies for that. As
necessary, Kamaria and I would update the list of adults she could contact if we were not
immediately available when she needed us.

   Right around 14, Kamaria received a text request for a picture of her in the shower.
The boy said he was going to send his shower pic after she sent hers. Thankfully,
something sparked his mom to pop in his room and scroll through his phone. She called
KJ and asked to speak to her parents. She knew she had no choice but to give me the
phone. I was more than undone by the whole text convo that took place, was grateful for
his mom's actions and call, and disappointed that KJ didn't immediately tell me what
was being asked of her.

   After her tears, my fussing, and the removal of phone privileges, I went to my room.
I calmed down and tried to figure out why she didn't come to me as much as we talk
about things. She clearly knew it wasn't appropriate. But then I remembered myself at
that age. I remembered the sweet secrets of excitement and anticipation inside a girl's
heart when some likes you. I remembered the uncertainty of what to do when presented
with new and daring concepts. Not that I liked the reasons at all, but I realized she and I
would continue to talk for years to come.

   Here are the facts about pornography:

- Once you see it, you can't unsee it. The images stick with you.

, it is illegal for you to even look at it.

...alsehood of what intercourse and intimacy was designed for.

...o one, not even someone your age, should be asking/encouraging you to look at porn or take pictures of your private parts and sending the picture to them.

- Any pictures you take and share electronically will FOREVER be in the cyber world and can be used against you if they are found, now and decades into the future.

- Viewing porn affects your mind, spirit, and your body.

- Be wise and be safe. Porn can be harmful to you now and in the future. Take care. Be safe. Be wise.

Journal Entry:

Chapter 8 – Safety

The condition of being protected from or unlikely to cause

danger, risk, or injury.[3]

In this global and mobile world we live in, it's more important than ever to be on your toes when it comes to personal safety. I'm not talking about being paranoid, rather about taking care of yourself, your surroundings, and your personal information. To this day, I still remind Kamaria of basic safety measures. It only takes a moment of carelessness to go from safety to being in desperate trouble. Yes, accidents happen, and mistakes are made, but control what you can while you are having fun. Make wise decisions about what you consider fun and who you can have the right kind of fun with.

Personal Safety: A general recognition and avoidance of possible harmful situations or persons in your surroundings.[16]

"My daughters, your daughters, our daughters deserve safety, protection and the freedom to make their own choices about their personal lives and their personal selves." -Carre Otis

Personal safety and physical safety are one in the same. Another of my famous quotes is "take care." While many people say this when they are departing someone's presence or ending a phone call or letter, I often said this to KJ to remind her to pay attention, to focus, to not be aloof. When we don't take care and pay attention to details, things can easily go wrong. I couldn't stress enough that it was Kamaria's responsibility to ensure she did her part to take care of her personal safety.

One of KJ's Christmas gifts when she was younger came with a unique name. When it came to teaching her about personal safety, I decided we would use that name as her code word. As she grew and became more independent: hanging with friends, walking home from school, or staying after school for activities I would occasionally ask for her code word, just to make sure she was being safe and to reminder her that I am always there. These reminders helped her to be more aware of her surroundings and actions.

I reminded her not to become too lax. Just because you have a cellphone or other technology, I don't want to always track you and yes, you can call me at any time, but I want to trust you. Whether you are with friends, family or alone, you must be mindful and aware of where you are, who you are with, and what's going on around you. To this day, the code word remains intact.

Journal Entry:

Internet Safety: Being safe online means individuals are protecting themselves and others from online harms and risks which may jeopardize their personal information, lead to unsafe communications, or even effect their mental health and wellbeing.[17]

"Internet has made the world a small town again." -Ana White

We all know and have heard the good, bad, and downright scary on and about the internet. And it is all true. We need to discuss personal safety in the virtual world. Not everything nor everyone is exactly what they appear or presents themselves to be.

When KJ was in middle school, having multiple home computers with internet access became increasingly common in many houses. However, I was not so sure about her having internet in her room. I wasn't sure she was ready to handle the level of access she would have, that she would not share personal information, and I was also concerned about those adults who pretend to be kids to prey on our children.

It was all still too new for me. As much as KJ said she would be safe, I wasn't ready to risk it. The rule was: whenever she needed the internet, she could use my computer in my workspace in the kitchen, but for school only. It was in an open area, where I can keep an eye on her internet activities.

Today, with phones, tablets, laptops, smartwatches, video games played with people worldwide, the dark web, trolls, cyber bullying…I could go on and on. I do not envy you when it comes to dealing with the internet and the safety of your children. I will say it again, Knowledge is Power.

I told KJ, between teaching you how to keep yourself safe and reminding you about the possibilities of predators trying to connect with you, there is so much to be leery of. We are not trying to keep you from enjoying your life, talking with friends, or even gaming (well, as long as it doesn't interfere with schoolwork or chores). We just want you to be safe, surf in moderation, and make wise choices.

Journal Entry:

Driving: The controlled operation and movement of a land vehicle, such as a car, truck, or bus.[18]

"Never drive faster than your guardian angel can fly." -Unknown

In a few short years, you will be driving! I bet you can hardly wait. Know that *driving is a privilege*, to be earned. It is not a right. Great responsibility comes with it. As much fun and freedom, you can have in a car, is as much danger and confinement you can have because of reckless use of that privilege. Poor decisions and carelessness can turn tragic for you, passengers, and innocent people around you.

No, I'm not overreacting. No, I am not being dramatic. I am keeping it real. Some parents watch how their children listen to and obey instructions, complete simple requests and tasks, and even how they handle riding a bike, as indicators of how they may be as new drivers. This was the case with KJ.

In elementary and middle school, we lived in a golf cart community. Lots of paths to schools, stores, and parks. Many families owned their own golf carts. We weren't one of those families.

However, we lived across the street from one of the lunchroom ladies from KJ's school and she simply loved KJ. When KJ was about 12, the lady told her she could borrow the golf cart from time to time. Of course, Kamaria knew she had to run the idea through me first. At the time, 11 or 12 was the driving age allowable on a golf cart with or without an adult. After weeks of begging, I finally told KJ we would go for a ride and she could drive. After going over all the instructions and safety precautions, she was beyond ready to drive, insisting she was ready, and she knew what to do.

You can see where this may be heading...can't you?! Things were going fine. She handled the curves well, followed the road signs, and slowed when there were walkers, joggers, or other carts to pass us. About 15 minutes into our adventure, there was a sharp curve. Instead of slowing down, she sped up. Instead of turning with control, she over-corrected. Instead of listening to my calm instructions, she heard me scream "STOP!" just as we hit a medium-sized tree.

Thankfully, no one was hurt nor flown from the cart (it had no seatbelts). The tree did sustain a minor ding, KJ was a bit shaken, and I was too! We sat there for a minute. Regrouped and then I asked what happened? She didn't have an answer. Going with the thought of getting right back on the horse when you fall off, I let her continue driving, slow and steady. I remembered that incident when she turned 15. So, I enrolled her in driver's ed and would take her to practice driving in large, empty parking lots for a while, before we ever got on the road!

Once you have your license, you will find that driving is fun. Enjoy the privilege, take care if the responsibility, and stay safe.

Journal Entry:

Motorcycles and Guys: No definition, but definitely need to address under safety!

"Note to self: Never ride a motorcycle in stilettos and a miniskirt." -Maggie Grace

Some may be wondering why this was a topic worth mentioning. Well, I will tell you. Kamaria's dad was a member of a motorcycle club. She spent a good part of her life around motorcycles. As she began to show interest in boys, I had to realize the possibility that she may interested in a boy who also rides motorcycles. Not something I would be a fan of. I have nothing against motorcycles. I just had something against my teenaged daughter on one with a teenaged boy. And especially one who wants to showoff for her attention! So, I decided before that time came to show and tell her a few things about young guys, motorcycles, and how often they take unnecessary risks.

Boys and young men have a feeling of invincibility. Too many times they believe "that will never happen to me," or "I'm too cool. Too fast. I know what I'm doing." This attitude and motorcycles don't mix. Whenever we would come across guys on motorcycles who were speeding, popping wheelies, weaving in and out of traffic or doing tricks on the highway or streets, I would be sure to point them out to her. I'd say, "this type of fun is not funny," or "these aren't the places to play like that." On other occasions she would hear, "it's all fun and games until someone gets hurt, or worse." We talked about her making wise choices by watching how boys behaved in other situations to help her determine their decision-making abilities. Just remember, cute and wise don't always go together.

Thankfully, I don't have a story to share about her early dating years, involving motorcycles. That was never an issue. WHEW!

Journal Entry:

Chapter 9 – ATOD

Alcohol, tobacco, and other drugs.[19]

It's easy to say, 'just say no!' But it's a whole different story when you are being pressed on every side by your peers, the cute boy you've had a crush on for forever, or you are feeling depressed and you're not sure what to do next. As parents, we can remember having those difficult preteen or teen experiences. And if your parent didn't have those experiences, I'm sure someone close to them did. It is vital to share these experiences with you.

You need to know that we weren't always 'old.' Additionally, you will come to appreciate the level of honesty we share with you. Hopefully, it will help strengthen the bonds of trust between us. Sharing these experiences also lets you know that it is possible to successfully ride the rollercoaster, that can easily be characterized as the teen years; get off; and walk into the future. And you know this to be true because we did it.

I had a few parents concerned that if they shared their experiences it may give their child a pass to do it and not get in trouble. I believe that is far from true. When I began sharing my experiences with Kamaria, I shared my reasons for or against 'indulging' in ATOD. I didn't make excuses, I kept it factual and I shared any consequences I may have suffered as a result of my decisions. I also set the tone and clear expectations I had of her regarding these matters. ATOD was one of the conversations we repeatedly had over the years.

Stress Management: the body's reaction to any change that requires an adjustment or response. The body reacts to these changes with physical, mental, and emotional responses.[24]

"Take a deep breath. It's just a bad day, not a bad life." -Unknown

The sources of stress can be positive or negative; they can be caused internally or externally. Stress is ANYTHING that causes a change in your body – thoughts, the doorbell, a text message, your grades…anything. There are four types of stress: Eustress, good stress, negative stress, and distress. Eustress is when we push ourselves to optimal performance. Think of an Olympic athlete who trains eight hours a day, eats lean meals and doesn't get enough rest all to have her best performance and win The Gold. Then there's good stress such as getting an A on your exam, making the varsity cheer team, or getting tickled by your little brother. Next, we have negative or distress, this is caused by things like, fighting with your parents, locking yourself out the house, or breaking your phone. Finally, there's wellness, which is the balance and harmony of the other three types of stress.

It's important to recognize how stress shows up in your body and the best ways to bring yourself back balanced. Kamaria heard me give talks on stress for a good part of her life, yet when her stress began to build at age 14, she was so caught up in her feelings she couldn't think clearly enough. This is something that can happen to all of us.

KJ began excessively worrying about national and international events and how they impacted people and her future. She stressed to the point of severe stomach pain, and to almost inconsolable tears at a moment's notice. KJ started carrying the weight of the world on her shoulders. We were able to address her stomach issues through medicine. However, her emotions weren't so easily calmed. Through prayer and what I know through my profession, I was led to an effective plan of action whenever her empathic emotions overtook her. And 'overtake' is the best word for what would happen: in the car, on the school bus, in the cafeteria, at night…

The first time this occurred was on the school bus heading to school. I received a call from one of KJ's friends, Lex (not her real name), frantic because KJ wouldn't stop crying. Now, KJ had just gotten on the bus 10 minutes prior, and when she left home she was fine. Lex told me KJ was crying hard, she couldn't stop to tell her what was going on. Lex put the phone to Kamaria's ear so I could speak with her, but she just kept crying.

I told her I would be at the school when the bus arrived. Steadily crying, just not as hard, KJ got in the car. She was able to let me know that no one had hurt her, and she wasn't in any pain. Once home, I had her take a long, warm shower, put on her comfy bathrobe, and then meet me on the sofa, where I had a cup of hot chamomile tea waiting.

We sat in silence for a while, she laid her head on my shoulder, and we sipped tea. I then asked her what was going on. Kamaria began listing: the country is running out of gas because pipelines are on fire or breaking and the making gas prices high, "they" are going to stop giving students loans so how will we pay from her college, the war in Iraq seems like it will never end, there are always mass shootings… at that point she started crying again.

I said, ok, keeping drinking your tea. I took some slow deep breaths and invited her to join me. I then started talking, providing some facts or clarity about some of the topics she listed. For the others, I told her I had no answers, but we could do our part to pray, be kind to others, and practice personal safety as best we can. We then sat in silence for a few more minutes, breathing deeply. I then sent her to her room to put on a new outfit so she could go back to school. This entire situation lasted about 90 minutes.

KJ's empathic experiences would occur every two to three months for the first year. When they occurred at school, I'd check her out for a "doctor's appointment," and we'd walk and talk it out at a nearby park. Each time, her recovery to balance was shorter than the time before. I helped KJ learn to recognize when the heaviness was building in her mind and body and discovered ways for her to shake them off.

Stress can show up as sweaty hands, rapid heartbeats, headaches, overeating or no appetite, oversleeping or insomnia, upset stomach, or clinched jaws to name a few bodily responses…it is individual response.

Too much negative stress causes tumors, ulcers, hair loss, weight gain or loss, depression, diabetes, high blood pressure and so much more. Distress can lead to disease. Ways to calm yourself range from deep breathing, dancing, playing sports, taking a nap for 30 to 60 minutes, walking, punching a pillow, listening to relaxing music or music that lifts your spirits. There are more ways to calm yourself, as this too is an individual response.

Listen to your body, take care of your mind, learn and practice self-care. Life is full of stressors, but with the right responses to them you can live in wellness.

A word about *depression.* PLEASE DO NOT SUFFER IN SILENCE. There are hotlines, prevention apps and websites you can find on your cellphone. Know that your feelings are real, but they are temporary. There are people and services to support you. Please REACH OUT 24/7. YOU MATTER. You are worthy.

Call: 1-800-622-4357

Text: HOME to 741741

Download: Moodpath APP

Journal Entry:

Drug Use & Substance Abuse: Recreational or excessive use of psychoactive drugs, such as alcohol, pain medications, or illegal drugs. It can lead to physical, social, or emotional harm[25].

"You can't change what's going on around you until you change what's going on inside you." -Unknown

"She fell. She crashed. She broke. She cried. She crawled. She hurt. She surrendered. And then...She ROSE again." -Helen's Journey

As parents, drugs and our children are one of our biggest concerns. As you become more independent and are influenced by your peers and the far-too-many forms of media that you have instant access to, drugs can creep in insidious ways. It makes preemptive attacks necessary. I started speaking with Kamaria about drugs around the age of 4.

We were in the car and the "just say no" PSA came on the radio. KJ began to ask what are drugs? Why do they want us to say no? What do drugs do? I answered as best I could for a 4-year-old. She left the conversation with the basic knowledge that drugs destroy your life and others that love you. Fast forward seven years, and the conversations were more in depth and hit closer to home.

Kamaria, like most people, has continuously and assuredly stated that she would never do drugs. And it is my hope and prayer that remains true for her entire life. But I don't know of nor have I ever heard of a substance user or abuser who set out to become addicted. My point is, there is no cut off age when people aren't at risk of addiction.

Prescription pain killers and alcohol are both legal substances that can easily be abused and cause you to become addicted, especially if you are under heavy stress.

During her middle and high school years, this subject was one she would often slyly roll her eyes to, sigh and say, "Mom, I know all about this. We talk about it in health class. Plus, we've had this talk multiple times and I told you I'm not going to do drugs." Ignoring her teenaged exasperation, I continued on.

I shared earlier how I wanted to be 'that mom,' have 'that house' that all the kids could feel at home in. One because I enjoyed the energy they brought to the house, but two because I would get first-hand knowledge of the what's, who's, when's and how's of Kamaria and her friends' lives. Like I stated, I could see which friends might not be the best friends for her due to the choices they made. A big concern with them was underaged drinking. That's because it's so readily available in many homes.

One weekend, one of my nieces by love (she was about 15 and KJ about 13), was hanging out with us when I decided to bring up the conversation about drug usage. Specifically, alcohol use and abuse. As I started talking, Roseanna said she couldn't wait to turn 21 so she could drink. She went on to say she had never really seen me drink, so she asked if I had ever been drunk. I told her I had not.

Neither girl thought I was telling the truth. I assured them I was and gave them the following reasons: aside from an occasional frozen drink, I never found a drink I really liked and so I stopped trying to find one. As for being drunk, I don't like to throw up. I always wanted to be aware of what was going on around me, and I have so much fun without drinking or getting drunk, it was never a real thought to me. Lastly, I shared that I may have been afraid that if I found a drink I liked, maybe I'd start to like it too much and couldn't stop.

They asked more questions, and I truthfully shared my college and adult experiences surrounding alcohol use and my inner circle. We ended that conversation with: 21 is the legal age because it is assumed that you are better able to drink more responsibly. That isn't always the case. In fact, you can be 90 years old and still not drink responsibly if you have an alcohol addiction.

Just because you can drink, doesn't mean you should drink. When you do decide to drink, make sure you are in a safe environment and around people who will really have your back. Everyone doesn't have the same alcohol tolerance levels...know yours. There is nothing wrong with drinking, but like everything, it should be done in moderation.

Journal Entry:

Smoking Cigarettes or Vaping: Smoking is the direct inhalation of tobacco smoke, the basis of major health hazards[25]. Vaping is the action or practice of inhaling and exhaling vapor containing nicotine and flavoring produced by a device designed for this purpose.[3]

"The best time to quit smoking was the day you started. The second best time to quit is today." -Unknown

I believe smoking was never an option for Kamaria. At an early age, she learned the story of her Poppa, my dad. He passed away at 53, from cancer, because of a smoking habit he started at the age of 12. Kamaria was three months old. When she was younger, she would cry because she never got to know him. We keep him alive by sharing stories and pictures. I am sure the two of them would have been thick as thieves!

"Every smoker has a story. So, before you say to him 'smoking kills,' I want you to know that something is already killing him." -Unknown

I always thought my dad started smoking because he thought it was cool. It wasn't until recently that I put together the real reason he started smoking and at such a young age. My grandfather, his dad, passed away earlier that year from tuberculosis. So, the above statement has a strong meaning for us. KJ's Poppa was deeply hurting inside because he lost his father. He lost his direction. Looking for connection to other guys he found it with a group who also smoked.

Most of my growing years, I tried, asked, and begged my dad to quit. He would try, time and again, but the addition was too strong. Back then they didn't have gums, patches, or 10-step programs. It was basically cold turkey.

While there are programs to help ease the habit of smoking, it is always best not to start. Providing safe spaces for open communication, creating memories, and genuinely connecting with family and friends are ways to reduce the opportunities for our children to start smoking.

To add to the use of cigarettes is the presence of vaping. Vaping was not around when KJ was in school. So, this wasn't a conversation we had. But it has since developed and become popular. Its makers started giving the vaping pens colors and designs. Far too many young people start vaping in middle school. They think it's a safe alternative to cigarettes and that it makes them look or be cool. Do not mistake the fact that vaping is extremely dangerous and will have health effects that science is just beginning to recognize. Providing healthy alternatives for connections, as well as ensuring our children know the facts about cigarettes and vaping are key to stemming the tide to decrease the smoking population.

Journal Entry:

Chapter 10 - Spirituality

The quality of being concerned with the human spirit or soul as

opposed to material or physical things; strong belief in God or in

the doctrines of a religion, based on spiritual apprehension

rather than proof[3].

I believe we are all spiritual beings having a human experience. Our spirits are the essence of who we are, our character, personality, our energy. It is not connected to a religion nor a particular faith. Our spirit is who we are at our core.

In sharing this overall concept with Kamaria, I presented it this way: have you ever been in a room when someone walks in and the whole room just seems to light up? There's laughter, smiles, all around good feelings. The person, and maybe it's you, works the room, seems to know everyone, and is greeted warmly or warmly greets others. Just thinking about that can make you smile, right? Then there's the person who enters the room and there seems to be an air of mystery, heaviness or darkness that surrounds them. Or maybe the energy in the room starts to decrease. That energy, high or low, is the person's spirit.

KJ understood what I was saying and shared a few experiences of her own, regarding people's energies. We are all connected. Our energies can vibe or feed off one another. Because of this, it is important for our girls to recognize and affirm their own spirit, protect their spirit when they are around those with heavier spirits, and learn ways to recapture their own spirit when it seems to be heavy. For me, this is where faith and perspective come in.

Faith: Complete trust or confidence in someone or something.

"Now faith is the assurance of things hoped for, the conviction of things not seen." -
Hebrews 11:1

Faith is a key component in my family's life. My mom's faith started developing at an early age. She passed that along to my sister and me, and I passed it along to my daughter. While our faith rests in God, others may have faith in a religion or something that is not considered a religion, it may be faith in yourself. I don't want you to be turned off by this talk because you believe differently. Again, knowledge is power and at some point in your life you will question and seek for faith in your own way.

KJ was raised in the church. She participated in all children's and youth activities, developed some of her best friendship, and regularly attend Sunday service. Around age seven or eight she started asking questions like: why do we believe what we do and not in another religion? How was my faith so strong when we can't see God? And how can she be sure its God speaking to her? When she turned 11, her questions grew deeper and our conversations lasted longer around specific instances or experiences she had. I was able to show ways in which KJ, unknowingly, put her faith in action, and ways in which God had provided or answered a prayer. I watched her faith mature and deepen into her own personal relationship.

There were certain things she knew for sure about her parents' faith and about her own. As a result, we were creating a healthy spiritual life for Kamaria. She had access to trusted adults who would answer the questions she had about life in general, and her purpose specifically. KJ was able to create healthy relationships with peers, both in and out of church. She knew when there were things she didn't want to or know how to share she could turn inward, and someone was listening.

One of the most pivotal tools KJ learned about her faith was that when situations came up that had her feeling hurt, confused, angry, or sad, she could call upon her faith to carry her through. Not as a 'magic pill,' but as something that had gotten her through before and would somehow get her through again. Her belief, understanding and our guidance helped to shape the values and character of the young woman she was developing into.

Church: A building for public worship and especially Christian worship[3].

Mosque: A Muslim place of worship.[3]

Temple: A building devoted to the worship, or regarded as the dwelling place, of a god or gods or other objects of religious reverence.[3]

Synagogue: The building where a Jewish assembly or congregation meets for religious worship and instruction.[3]

Religion: A particular system of faith and worship[10].

"I was thinking, if I cheated on my fears, broke up with my doubts, got engaged to my faith, I can marry my dreams." - Beyonce

Journal Entry:

Perspective: Life perspective is the way people see life, including the way they approach life and all there is in their personal experience. In this life, few things are absolutely right or wrong[29].

"Remove those 'I want you to like me' stickers from your forehead and, instead, place them where they truly will do the most good – on your mirror!" -Susan Jeffers

"Look at everything as though you were seeing it either for the first or last time. Then your time on earth will be filled with glory." -Betty Smith

"Sometimes you're so focused on your own stuff that you forget other people have problems too." -Madison Iseman

Your perspective is 100% real to you! But as the definition above says, nothing is absolutely right or absolutely wrong. Our perspectives, our viewpoints are formed from our own unique experiences. No two people see anything the exact same way. This is the underlying basis for arguments, disagreements, fights and all out wars. We can spend so much time trying to get others to see things 'our way,' when at best, they can only have a similar viewpoint or understanding of what we are attempting to show them. Knowing where you stand on things is important. Providing grace and space for others to share their perspectives is also important, especially if it is someone whose relationship you value.

KJ has a slightly older cousin who visited every summer. They looked forward to their times together every year. However, when KJ was 11 and Jamie was 13, the visit summer was different. Jamie was secretive, on her phone with her friends back home, talking about boys, and wanted to be left alone. In KJ's words, Jamie was rude and mean. I believe Jamie even said something like, 'I don't want to play that, I'm not a kid.'

Kamaria wasn't impressed and didn't want to spend time with her anymore. I told KJ that Jamie is a teenager now and has different interests than you. She then replied, well Jamie doesn't have to be so mean. I agreed and suggested that she remember how she is feeling now, so that when she turned 13 she remember how she is feeling now and make sure her younger cousins didn't feel the same way. I shared with KJ that 13 is a special age when you feel older and more mature. I told her she will see things a little differently at that age, as you change from being a kid to a teen.

In conflict, keeping perspectives in mind can be important. *When Kamaria had a disagreement with someone, I encouraged her to take a step back, listen, and try to see the incident from the other person's perspective, as much as possible. Now, that doesn't mean that you will agree or change your position, but it means that you give them the chance to have their say. Kamaria would share that this wasn't always easy to do, sometimes it worked, sometimes not, and sometimes she didn't try because she was either to upset or didn't care what they had to say. And that's fair enough.*

The points that I want to leave with you with are: there is often more than one way to view a thing, that it's ok to change your position as long as you maintain your integrity and it is in alignment with your values, and lastly, that being open to other points of view are the way you grow.

Journal Entry:

Chapter 11 - Life

The ability to grow, change, etc., that separates plants and

animals from things like water or rocks; the period of time when

a person is alive; the experience of being alive[26].

This is all we get. Right here, right now. So, make it count. Live your life full and free. Know that there is no one else, ever, who is exactly like you, therefore, no one can do what you were born to do. The world needs you to show up, to fall and get back up, to succeed and win. You are the leader of your own life. Lead the way.

Authenticity: Real or genuine; not copied or false; true and accurate[10].

"Doubt is a killer. You just have to know who you are and what you stand for." - J. Lo

Living in your truth may be one of the most challenging characteristics for you to grasp during these preteen and teen years. You are just beginning to grow into your own and find your voice. And as you do, you are confronted with internal and external challenges to your newly discovered self-hood. This is such a valuable concept and trait to learn.

I will admit, as all adults can attest, discovering and living in your own authenticity is not always easy, and it is a continuous process. We have to learn who we truly are in different seasons of our life and sometimes in different situations within the same season. It is the nature of experiencing, growing, and learning. I believe is starts with spending time with yourself, listening to your heart, and expressing yourself in written or spoken words, dance, music, sports, art, or even math.

Kamaria often had a busy schedule. Between school, sports, social activities and spending every other weekend with her dad and siblings, she was on the go. My best friend called her the 'go baby' from an early age. Around 4th or 5th grade I realized she needed to learn how to unplug and unwind. That's when I instituted 'Stay at home Saturday's.' Basically, once we got home on Friday the car was not moving again until Sunday morning.

On those days she could stay in her pj's and chill, doing whatever she wanted to do if it did not include us driving anywhere. The goal was for her the learn to enjoy spending time with herself. Occasionally, a friend from the neighborhood could come over, but mostly, it was just her. It took a minute for her, and me, to get the hang of not doing anything. But once she got it, she enjoyed the down time.

When you take time away from the continual noise and motion of life, it is easier to center yourself. You can hear your own thoughts, recognize your feelings, and learn to express yourself in creative ways. I have found, and therefore, taught KJ that this is how you discover who you are to yourself. Once you do that, you can discover who you are in relationship to your friends, family and in the experiences you have. All relationships develop from the one you have with yourself.

Being authentic and standing for your values can be scary, especially when your friends are doing the opposite of what you stand for. While they may try to convince you to join them, true friends will respect your decision and remain friends without judging you. The more they see you walking in what you've said, the better they will become at understanding the type of person you are growing into. Be authentically yourself, as often as you can. Because that's truly all you can ever really be.

Journal Entry:

Surviving vs. Thriving: Surviving is a grim struggle, just barely getting by. Thriving is living and thinking abundantly[2].

"You can never live your life looking at yourself from someone's point of view." - Penelope Cruz

Thriving is being hopeful, having a positive outlook, taking healthy risks, having dreams, and moving towards those dreams. We are all meant to thrive! Though, some days, surviving is the best we can do. And that's ok. We can have low energy, off days, and down days. However, it's important to keep in mind that those days will pass. Thriving days should outweigh the surviving days.

I tried to ensure KJ had new and different experiences growing up. I wanted her to have a broader view of what life was like outside of our suburban community. She tried different sports, was part of various social activities, attended diverse cultural events, sampled lots of different ethnic foods, and was blessed to travel to different parts of the country, and even to Europe with other middle schoolers from across the state.

We used to hang out at the airport to watch the planes land and take off. I would ask her where she thought the plane was coming from or where it was going, what the weather would be like when they arrived, and why the passengers might be traveling. Starting at a young age, I encouraged her to dream, to make up bedtime stories, and to stretch her imagination. When she was around 12, I began teaching her how to goal set, plan, and create her first vision board. We talked about goal setting and planning in Chapter 5.

Through the numerous outings, events, and occasions, Kamaria developed a healthy adventure for living. No dream or idea was too big to conceive, talk about, plan (even if it was only a plan), or try out. This is my idea of thriving. Not stifling your creativity about what your life can and will look like. Finding the joys in each day from laughing during lunch with your friends to a wonderful weekend trip with the family; from sleeping in on a snow day to passing that tough exam; or from seeing the friendly dog that greets you as you walk home from school to the being selected first chair. Whether small or large, thriving starts in your mind and continues in your actions.

Your thoughts dictate your emotions, and your emotions lead to your actions. What you do today sets you up for the life you will live tomorrow. Thriving is an option...a decision... and an intention. Even on the toughest days, it's ok to acknowledge your emotions. In fact, it's healthy to do that. After you acknowledged your sadness, hurt, anger...Give herself a set amount of time to feel all of it.

Once that time was up, move on to something else to clear your mind of the situation. When your emotions are under control, revisit the situation and find the benefit or lesson, if any, in it. Lastly, as I shared with you at the beginning of this topic, this too shall pass. No matter how big the problem, life is ultimately amazing! Keep moving, don't get stuck. Life will take its twists and turns, but that is the nature of living. Keep striving, keep climbing, keep conquering. Learning these lessons will help build your muscles to endure and overcome.

Journal Entry:

Volunteering & Community Service: Freely offer to do something[3].

"You only have what you give. It's by spending yourself that you become rich."-
Isabel Allende

Contrary to popular belief, life doesn't simply revolve around you. It is not all about us. Individually, that is. It is about us collectively. Some of the activities and events Kamaria grew up participating in included feeding the homeless, donating personal items to those in need, reading to children at the local children's hospital, painting classrooms, cleaning up yards, giving manicures to female residents in nursing homes during the annual ML King, Jr. Day of Service, or planting flowers to help beautify a neighborhood. Acts of service to help others - whether you know them or not - just because it's the right thing to do, not only benefits them, but they benefit you as well.

We just finished talking about the tough places that life can take you. Well, it has been said, and KJ and I have found this to be true, when you do something nice for someone else, it helps get you out of the down mood you were in. When we extend our support to lift someone else, we can't help but to lift ourselves. We do not live in this world alone and we cannot make it through life alone. We need each other. The person or community you serve today may be the ones who support or serve you tomorrow.

A few more benefits can be had from volunteering. When you extend yourself in service to others, it gives you something to be proud of. It says something positive about your character when you are being considered for a scholarship, college entry or a job position, and when you are joined in your activity by family or friends, it creates a special kind of bond and memories you will share forever.

More than a decade after traveling to Jamaica with a youth group on a mission's trip, KJ still remembers the smiles and hugs from the young school children she worked with. She can recall the food, the scenery, and the friendships she made. Community service helps you to be the best version of yourself.

Journal Entry:

Leader vs. Follower: Leadership is the art of persuasion—the act of motivating people to do more than they ever thought possible in pursuit of a greater good[27]. Follower is one in the service of another; one that follows the opinions or teachings of another[10].

"Leadership is about helping others realize their potential and inspiring them to work with you to achieve a shared vision for the future." -Kathy Mazzarelli

"True leaders keep pushing forward even when there's no carrot dangling in front of them."-Unknown

"A leader is only as good as what he or she can achieve through other people."-Unknown

Being a leader or a follower are not mutually exclusive distinctions. You don't have to be either or, you can be both depending upon the situation. Additionally, you can be both at the same time. The fact is that we are all leaders of our own lives. At least we should be. And this is an important fact I wanted to drive home with Kamaria.

I can remember one situation as if I had gotten the call today. It was around 4 p.m. on a Friday when KJ was in her 5th grade chorus practice, when I, the PTA VP, received a call from the principal that my daughter was in her office. I will attempt to give you the short version! After having multiple chorus teachers with their own teaching styles in a short period of time, most students, including my beloved KJ, stopped taking chorus seriously. They were goofing off and not listening nor following instructions. Having enough, the chorus teacher told the principal, who decided to address the students.

After the principal finished her lecture and left the class, KJ took it upon herself to say, not so quietly, "we don't have to listen to her. She's not the boss of me." The principal's son, who sat near KJ, heard her. When he got home, his mom asked how the class was after her 'talk,' he told her how some behaved and what was said but didn't name names. Until she pressed him, that is.

So, I get the call that KJ was in her office and had admitted her words. The principal shared that the punishment would be sweeping the school's hallways for two days after school. A few things: 1) I wasn't thrilled that KJ was questioned without my knowledge, 2) let's keep it real, being on the PTA, I was embarrassed that my daughter was disrespectful (1 of the top 2 things I will never tolerate), and 3) I was livid that she even thought it was ok to say that out loud! Sensing my anger, she assured me that she taken care of the situation. To which, I assured her that she had her punishment, and I would have mine. Then I asked to speak to my child, and assured KJ that I was on my way to deal with her.

The rapid-fire earful I gave Kamaria went something like this: "Who do you think you are to say someone isn't the boss of you? In fact, it's her school, so she IS the boss! Are you a gang leader? Cause that's what gang leaders do – they get people all geeked up to go against authority in negative ways. Are you the leader of a gang I should know about? Cause that's not the type of leader we are raising you to be! But since you are obviously confused as to what type of leader you are, I tell you what you are going to do. You will write two letters of apology. One to the principal for being disrespectful and rude. The other to the chorus teacher and the class. The last one you will read out loud and in front of the entire class... Mortified and embarrassed, that's exactly what she did.

Once I was calm, I reminded KJ that she is a leader of her own words and actions, and of some of her friends who follow her. I told her it is her responsibility to do the right thing, even when it's not the popular thing. I further reminded her that the right thing should be done whether I am there or not, and not because she may get caught, but because someone is always watching her. In our faith, that someone is God. In a practical meaning, you never know who's watching, snapping pics or taking videos that you may get caught up in.

Leaders lead by example. Leaders accept responsibility. Leaders work alongside their team. Leaders motivate and inspire. Followers lead their own lives and have responsibility for their own actions and words too. Followers should not follow blindly. Followers must keep their own thoughts, values, and integrity intact, so they don't get caught up in straight foolishness!

Journal Entry:

Family & Heritage: Family: 1a: the basic unit in society traditionally consisting of two parents rearing their children: b. any of various social units differing from but regarded as equivalent to the traditional family; 2a: a single-parent family: b: spouse and children; 3a: a group of individuals living under one roof and usually under one head: b. a group of persons of common ancestry; 4a: a people or group of peoples regarded as deriving from a common stock: b: a group of people united by certain convictions or a common affiliation[10]. **Heritage** can refer to practices or characteristics that are passed down through the years, from one generation to the next[4].

"As for my girls, I'll raise them to think they breathe fire." -Jessica Kirkland

"Be clothed in strength, and dignity, and be proud of your heritage." -Miss Fiyah

Growing up, Kamaria had to often spend time around one of her adult male relatives who didn't understand the ever-changing life and times of preteen girls. Because he was not blessed with sisters, only had brothers, he could not wrap his mind around why she and her friends wanted to hangout in the kitchen instead of outside or in her bedroom; why they shrieked and squealed about nothing, yet almost everything; or why one minute there was laughter and then next inconsolable tears.

KJ thought he was just grumpy. I told her that while he may seem overly grumpy, he was family and he loved her in his own way. I suggested that she try to find common ground and a way to positively interact with him. That while his attitude and ways were different than what she would like, she would meet people throughout her life who would have the same mannerisms, conversations, and thoughts as this relative. Bosses, coworkers, and classmates aren't always easy to deal with.

I shared that people come into our lives, especially in our family, to teach us how to best relate with others. If she learns how to best interact with him, she could use these lessons when she came across someone like him in the future.

Our family members, from those in our home to those we see regularly, are our most important and influential classmates and teachers. Our homes and communities are our natural learning environments. Learning the lessons of healthy relationships, healthy conversations, and healthy boundaries, along with what is not healthy, and other vital lessons, prepare you for interacting in our world. You cannot choose your family, but you can choose to learn the lessons they teach you about others and yourself and how to grow through and from them.

Your heritage is your family lineage, your tribe, sect, your people, your background, where you family is from. There is a lot to be said for one's heritage. Some people are proud of theirs, while others don't know anything about their ancestors. While you are uniquely you, there are traits and characteristics in your family history that just might interest you. Contact your oldest living relative and interview them.

One final thing about family. Family is not just those whom you are related to by blood. There are wonderful and loving relationships we have with our family by love. These are the people we choose to be in our lives. Those we give front row seats to in the story of our lives. They are there by privilege, not right. Some of these connections may be closer than those you have with some of your bloodline. Just like KJ, you may have several aunts, uncles, cousins, and grandparents by love, who have and who continue to help guide your life.

No matter, by blood or by love, family is important. Family is growth. Family is falling out. Family is reconnecting. Family is forgiveness. Family is hurt feelings. Family is laughing until you cry and crying until you laugh. Family is loud. Family is sitting in silence. Family is who and what you make it.

Journal Entry:

Chapter 12 - Money

A generally accepted, recognized, and centralized medium of exchange in an economy that is used to facilitate transactional trade for goods and services[28].

Everyone talks about having money and spending money daily; but few people talk about money as a tool that everyone needs to learn how to use effectively, safely and wisely. As parents, we want you to grow up to be independent, successful, and productive citizens. We want you to walk into adulthood and make it.

We know the financial realities and struggles that can come with that walk into adulthood, but for some reason, as parents, we often don't fully equip you with life lessons that we learned from our relationships with money. Now is the time. We need to teach you money management basics. DISCLAIMER: I am NOT a financial professional, expert, nor wiz, nor do I play one on TV! But there are plenty out there when you want to get more details.

Rich vs. Wealthy: Rich people spend a lot of money, but wealthy people save
and invest much of their money[28]. **Wealth** measures the value of all the assets of worth owned by a person, community, company, or country. Wealth is determined by taking the total market value of all physical and intangible assets owned, then subtracting all debts[28].

"It's not the money I'm after. It's the freedom. My goal is to live life on my own terms." -Debbie Roy

In the all-access world of smart phones and the internet, being rich is displayed as the end all, be all of truly living. Flashing cash and cards, jewelry, fast cars, hot clothes, trips all around the world are the envy of wide-eyed preteens who dream of living that lifestyle. But the truth, as adults know it, is that most people don't live that way, and that money is not the road to unlimited happiness nor a fulfilled life.

Now, don't get me wrong, money is very important to have. It allows us to attain needs and wants, and it allows us to support causes outside of ourselves. Learning how to use your money to make more money is a vital lesson for everyone to know. As Debbie Roy stated in the above quote, money allows you to have a certain level of freedom and self-determination. Money gives you choices on what you can and cannot eat, where you can and cannot live, and the type of comfort you can and cannot create for yourself.

When I introduced the rich vs. wealth topic to KJ, I asked her which she'd rather be. She quickly and initially responded "rich." When I asked her why, she said so she could buy things, including a house in the mountains for me (such a sweetie!). Then she thought about it and asked were there any real difference in the two.

I explained that rich can come and go very easily, rich is shallow money. However, wealth is deeper, lasts longer, grows, is credit-worthy, and provides far more options for your life and the lives of your children's, children's, children. If mismanaged, wealth can disappear as well. Wealth can come from being rich or from wise spending or investing small amounts. After hearing this, she preferred to be wealthy, but still said I could have my mountain retreat!

Rich can also be looked at as an emotional state of being, and wealth as a state of mind. Your relationship with money, spending habits, and ability to control impulsive wants and desires are mindsets that can be learned and cultivated to increase your wealth. I taught my daughter this through delayed gratification, which we'll discuss more in the next section.

Journal Entry:

Money Management: Is the process of budgeting, saving, investing, spending, or otherwise overseeing the capital usage of an individual or group[28].

"If you take control of your finances today, then you won't be a victim of them tomorrow."-Emily G. Stroud

Learning how to plan your money: budget, save, spend, invest and even donate wisely are lessons that are never completely mastered. As financial systems evolve, and as your needs and wants change, you have to adjust your plans and may have to seek the help of a financial professional or take a money management course.

I remember having Kamaria help me create a budget for a trip we would be taking in the summer. You can gain a better understanding of what it cost to run our house for a month, what money we had flexibility in the amount we spent, and what money we could have to play with during our family vacay. Her normal random requests to go shopping, out to eat, or for me to pick up something at the gas station nearly stopped so that we could have maximum opportunities for activities during our trip.

Another money management lesson came between December and February. Having a birthday that's not too long after Christmas, why don't you save most of the money, you might receive as a Christmas gift until after your birthday. This would allow you to see if the item you wanted to purchase would come as a birthday gift or if you could add any birthday money with the holiday money towards what you wanted. She did not really like waiting, who does? She wanted to spend 'her' money but was always excited when she was able to add to it and then make her purchase.

One of the key money principles this taught her was delayed gratification. Many times, due to the delay in her spending, the item she wanted would be on sale by the time she could buy it. Her extra money allowed her to buy something else or add more to her savings account.

You will also learn to manage money with your allowance and your bank account. KJ was required to save, give an offering to the church, and plan for any purchases above $25. I even had her attend a money management workshop for kids. Like me, you may not be a financial wiz, but having a strong foundational knowledge to build on as you moved into adulthood is a good start to independence.

Journal Entry:

Stewardship: Is the conducting, supervising, or managing of something; especially the careful and responsible management of something entrusted to one's care[10].

"Breathe. Let go. And remind yourself that this very moment is the only one you have for sure." -Oprah

Dear Parents, we are stewards of our own lives, of the lives entrusted to us through relationships, and of the items we have in our possession. As stewards, we are to take good care of what we have, to pass on what we no longer have use for or that which can be shared out of our overflow with others. This is one of the primary lessons Kamaria was raised with. And I am grateful that it is a lesson she embraced very easily.

Everything that I talk about in this journal, that I've shared with Kamaria and I've now shared with you, and everything you will or have shared with your daughter in these conversations is about stewardship. We each have been entrusted with these treasured gifts to shape, nurture, guide, correct and inform. The gift of our children. It is our sole responsibility to raise them to be healthy, thriving adults. I have chosen to share with you one of the ways I carried out this responsibility. In having these discussions, I was able to teach KJ how to steward herself in all areas of her life. She continues to grow into a conscientious and compassionate steward.

I am not a perfect parent and I don't have all the answers. Kamaria isn't a perfect daughter, and these conversations did not always go smoothly. I stuttered and tripped over words. But these conversations provided a safe place for us to talk, ask questions, find answers together, and develop a bond that I claim will withstand anything. I hope you have found it helpful and encouraging to begin or continue your own conversations.

Blessings,

Dr. Lisa

Journal Entry:

Topic of Your Choice to Repeat

A Letter to Our Daughters

First, I thank you for being here. Thank you for being open to the conversations, especially the hard and embarrassing ones. Next, I hope you know this, but just in case you don't... YOU ARE POWERFUL!

You are POWERFUL just as YOU ARE!

You grow more powerful each time you smile, you create, you imagine, you cry. You grow more powerful each time you believe in yourself, you believe in the good in others, you speak your truth, and you walk with your head up. You grow more powerful each time you stand up for yourself, and you stand for those who can't stand for themselves.

You are ENOUGH! The pieces you need for things to come together will fall in place at the right time, just as they are supposed to.

You are VALUABLE. You are WORTHY. You BELONG here. You FIT in. You have a PLACE. You have PURPOSE.

You, all of you, with your inner brilliance and your outer shine, is who you have been waiting for. You are who the world has been waiting for. You have been and always will be there for you.

Honor YOU. Trust YOU. Love YOU. Learn YOU. Re-discover YOU.

When you fall, get back up, learn the lesson, try again.

When you get hurt, feel the pain, name the pain, heal from the pain, trust again.

When you are confused, get still, breathe, rest, get up, take it one step at a time.

YOU are POWER. YOU are ENOUGH. YOU are VALUABLE.

I believe in you.

Blessings and love,

   Dr. Lisa

Appendix A

ABSOLUTELY ENOUGH!

Tell me when does it stop?

When do we declare our spot?

When do we reach for the top

of our own mountains and shout...

"I AM ENOUGH!"

I'm just askin' when?

When do we make our own sun rise and set?

When do we play our own game and bet

on ourselves to win and stop let-

ting ours determine the rules and parameters and

we just sit back with regret?

I'm just askin' when?

"When will I BE ENOUGH?"

ENOUGH for myself?

ENOUGH for you?

ENOUGH for them?

ENOUGH for the job?

ENOUGH for the world?

Well, I tell you what – I take my stand!

I declare I am in demand

in my own life, I command

all the best and rest of me to comprehend

that "I AM ABSOLUTELY ENOUGH!"

With my flaws and scars

I set my goals for the stars.

In my own right I have all I need to be

who I am right now and in the future.

"I AM ENOUGH!"

Dr. Lisa T. Sistrunk (2013)

Appendix B

The Girlfriends' Club

I created "The Girlfriends' Club" for my daughter and five of her peers. The girls ranged in age from six to nine. We met every two to three weeks on a Saturday, and their mothers had to participate as well. This wasn't difficult, as we were all friends and associates already. How they were raising their children was in line with how we were raising Kamaria.

We went to plays, the zoo, movies, to eat at all kinds of eateries to teach the girls how to conduct themselves, sporting events, and rodeos. There was a small decorative box we carried with us. The box contained strips of paper with questions, statements, or just topics. The girls took turns pulling strips and reading its contents. We would discuss whatever was pulled. This allowed us to hear what our daughters' thoughts and opinions, helped us to add perspective and the insight that comes with wisdom and experience. There was nothing off-limits, from how to give a firm handshake to creating your own style.

It was a wonderful time for us all. I hope you create your own friends club and have a wonderful time too!

Reference List

1. www.wewaonthenet.com
2. www.psychologytoday.com
3. www.oxfordlanguages
4. www.vocabulary.com
5. www.study.com
6. www.greatergood.berkeley.edu
7. www.uhs.berkeley.edu
8. www.loveisrespect.org
9. www.habitsforwellbeing.com
10. www.merriam.webster.com
11. www.thebalancesmb.com
12. www.urbandictionarycom
13. www.healthyplace.com
14. www.gaycenter.org
15. www.eeoc.gov
16. www.etsu.edu
17. www.blognationalonlinesafety.com
18. www.definitions.net
19. www.acronyms.thefree.dictionary.com
20. www.askdifference.com
21. www.collinsdictionary.com
22. www.ncbi.nlm.nih.gov
23. www.streetspiration.com.ng
24. www.myclevelandclinic.org
25. www.medicenet.com
26. www.google.com
27. www.medium.com
28. www.investopedia.com
29. www.lifehack.org
30. www.medicalnewstoday.com
31. https://www.ny.gov/teen-dating-violence-awareness-and-prevention/what-dating-abuse

Made in the USA
Columbia, SC
24 June 2021

40289797R00087